MY LIFE IN CARTOONS

PAUL DRIESSEN

MY LIFE IN CARTOONS

AT BAY press

Winnipeg

My Life in Cartoons

Design and layout by Lucas c Pauls.

Published by At Bay Press May 2024.

Library and Archives Canada cataloguing in publication is available upon request.

ISBN 978-1-998779-37-6

Printed and bound in Canada.

This book is printed on acid free paper that is 100% recycled ancient forest friendly (100% post-consumer recycled).

First Edition

10 9 8 7 6 5 4 3 2 1

atbaypress.com

Table of Contents

To my parents

PREFACE

About a year ago, I started a correspondence with three of my old schoolmates, friends I had been close to during my school days and with whom I had lost touch after we graduated and went in different directions.

Since we were all nearing our 80s, and almost the only thing I knew about them was that they were still alive, I was curious to find out not only how they had conducted their lives over the last 60 years of adulthood, but also what their early childhood had been like, the nest they came from.

I was glad to hear that they shared my interest, and although they told me a lot about their upbringing, family life and careers, thus rekindling our friendship, I realized that part of what I really enjoyed about the exchange was looking back at my own history and that of my parents, which, when compared to most of my contemporaries, appeared to have been quite an adventurous one.

Being a writer and cartoonist, when At Bay Press in Winnipeg proposed to do this book, I found it quite exciting to write down all the events that stood out in my memory. And, next to some photographs of my past, I enjoyed digging up a whole bunch of cartoons to illustrate the course of my life.

Lately, just by coincidence, I was reading some books which were based on memoirs: Motherland by Paul Theroux and Moonglow by Michael Chabon, two books written in a style way beyond my own writing skills, of course, but both very inspiring in their approach to narrating their lives.

As memories go, over the years they often create a life of their own, slightly different from the reality. So forgive me for sometimes wandering off; this document is how I experienced the journey of my life.

BEGINNINGS

It's a curious thing that despite my parents' lack of understanding of the visual arts, I became a visual artist.

Looking back, this always surprises me because my parents were very interested in culture. They both played piano, loved music, literature, theatre and dance. My mother wrote theatre plays and composed songs she would play on the guitar and make us sing along.

Even during the difficult years of the war, when I was three and my sister was four, our mother recorded our voices, singing the songs she wrote especially for us. Unfortunately, the old phonograph recording got lost during the many journeys my family undertook.

☆ ☆ ☆

My father was born in Rotterdam in 1904. His father, who had a wholesale business of fruit and vegetables, moved trainloads of his produce between Rotterdam and Berlin. Consequently, the family lived alternately in each of those cities for long periods of time.

My grandfather was less interested in the education of his three children than his enterprise, so the children often moved countries and schools, and as a result, my father was moved back to Berlin just before graduation and never finished his much-desired Dutch schooling.

When he was nine years old, my father saw the Kaiser of Germany, the King of England and the Tsar of Russia riding by, while he stood to attention. The year was 1913, the place was Berlin, and the occasion was a parade in honour of the wedding of the daughter of the German Emperor Wilhelm II.

Berlin wedding parade, 1913. My father is one of the 9-year-olds in the crowd.

When the Great Depression hit Germany in 1929, Hitler saw his chance, and the rise of the Nazi party began. Fortunately, during the 30s, my father was able to keep an administrative job at an international food company and helped to provide for his parents and his younger siblings. He was even able to pay for the passage of his younger brother Paul to travel to the Dutch East Indies, a Dutch colony full of opportunities for young adventurers at the time. The local population was less happy with the arrival of the budding entrepreneurs from far away Holland, of course.

When the Japanese forged an alliance with the German Nazi regime and occupied Indonesia, my Uncle Paul, who had done some sabotage to obstruct the invaders, was captured, tortured and shipped to a concentration camp in Japan where one day, he told me later, he heard a terrific "boom." We figured that it must have been one of the atomic bombs which were dropped on Japan.

When the war was over, Uncle Paul returned to Holland and lived till the ripe old age of 104, though recurring nightmares from the terrible things done to him followed him the rest of his life.

My mother was born in the city of Nijmegen in the east of the Netherlands, two days after her father's funeral. My grandmother, who was left on her own with four very young children during a time when government social support was virtually nonexistent, and women were not much valued in the job market, somehow managed to find employment and give her children a decent education. My mother acquired a teacher's degree, and being an adventurous young woman in the mid-30s, she accepted a position as the teacher of the children of the newly appointed Dutch consul in Berlin.

It was at the Dutch Club in Berlin where she met my father. They married in 1938, and my sister was born in April of the next year. Later that year, when the German troops threatened to invade the Netherlands, my father, who was a reserve officer in the Dutch army, was called back to Holland to fight the aggressors. My mother, pregnant with me, followed with my sister.

My parents' wedding picture. They are sitting together second from right.

I was born on March 30, 1940, one and a half months before the German army invaded the Netherlands. During the four days of battle between the poorly armed Dutch army and the heavily armed Germans, my father's division was encamped in Dordrecht, close to where the first heavily armed German paratroopers descended.

There was some heavy and uneven fighting going on, and I'm always surprised to hear that the Dutch took quite a few German prisoners. A large group of those prisoners were put on a barge on the river which streamed past Dordrecht and sailed to England. When the war in Holland ended after four days of fighting, and my father was arrested, he was accused of having eliminated this group of missing prisoners and put on trial. Being able to defend himself in German and explain what really happened saved his life.

After the Dutch defeat, the German occupation of the Netherlands began. We moved to Breda, a city in the southern province of Brabant, and although I was too young to be aware of it, life was poor, and we had very little to eat. I still vaguely remember my dislike of the daily porridge of bread soaked in water. And by contrast, the delight of the taste of white bread and chocolate dropped from planes when we were liberated. But times were not all bad. My mother read stories to us and taught us songs. We played in the garden in front of the house where we stayed and sometimes spent sunny days in the moorlands of Brabant, sleeping in the heather (still my favourite undergrowth) and bathing in the fens.

My first strong memory as a three-year-old is that while my parents were dozing off next to one of these fens, I crept to its edge, stepped into the water and walked along the bottom of the pond. I remember looking up to the surface, trying to follow a branch floating above my head. The next thing I remember is that my father had pulled me out, and I was choking and crying on his lap.

Since we lived south of what the Dutch call the Big Rivers, the Meuse, and the Waal, we were liberated by Polish and Canadian regiments in October 1944. I still remember hiding in the cellar, hearing sounds of shooting in the streets, which stopped abruptly, followed by silence. Then, after a little while, we heard heavy footsteps approach, stopping on top of the trapdoor above us. When it was opened, my parents uttered a sigh of relief when not a German soldier, but a Polish member of the liberating forces looked down at us, a big grin on his face.

Me and my sister in 1943.

We were lucky to be liberated in 1944, for in the terrible cold winter that followed, what the Dutch called the Hunger Winter, the Allies couldn't cross the big rivers because of heavy resistance from the German army on the other side. Thousands of Dutch citizens north of the rivers under German occupation died of hunger and cold.

After an initial jubilant atmosphere, the Netherlands, like all countries devastated by the war, must have been a depressing place. Much of the country lay in ruins and particularly Rotterdam, the native town of my father, was heavily bombed. So, when there came a rather unexpected offer to leave Holland and go elsewhere, my parents didn't hesitate for long, before they accepted.

The Dutch, related to the Tsar through the marriage of Anna Paulowna to their Crown Prince William II in 1816, had broken off all contacts with Russia when the Soviets came into power and executed the Russian royal family. However, when Stalin joined the Allies, the Dutch renewed their relationship with the Russian government and, in 1942, set up their embassy in Moscow.

During the tedious years under the German occupation, my father, who had always been interested in Russia, had distracted himself by studying the Russian language. Through my mother's former employer, the Dutch diplomat, my parents heard that the Dutch embassy in Moscow had an opening for an 'attaché à l'ambassade', basically an administrator who could organize social and cultural events.

It was a young and small embassy my family moved to; first, my father in the winter of 1946, followed later that year by my mother, sister, younger brother, and me, then seven years old. Although the photograph might not show it, we all had happy memories of the three years we spent in Moscow.

Driessen family in Moscow (I'm on the right).
We clearly didn't understand the Russian word for 'cheese' at the time.

When I was eight years old, on the first of May 1948, standing on the balcony of the American embassy in Moscow and looking through binoculars towards the Red Square, I saw Stalin saluting the tanks of the red army rolling by.

The 40s under Stalin were dangerous times for the Russians. His paranoid views sent millions of citizens to Siberia and death, and therefore, contact with foreigners like us was better avoided. It was one of the reasons we couldn't go to Russian schools.

Fortunately, my mother was a teacher. During our three-year-stay, she prepared us, as well as the two ambassador's children for the education system in Holland, where we, in all likelihood, would continue our schooling. I remember fondly the many hours my mother read to us from the small supply of children's books our grandmother sent to us. These reading classes instilled our later love of literature and writing.

However, we were not surrounded by kids, as most children our age were going to school. Most of the time, we were left to ourselves, playing in the large attic on top of the embassy or in the small garden in the back. We never wandered out in the street, as two armed soldiers guarded the entrance of the embassy. I was a little boy full of imagination, and I was often by myself, creating my own fantasy world. I attribute my ability to come up with original ideas for my films to those years of being rather isolated from conventional day-to-day life.

But then again, my ideas were never based on the visual world around me or things one sees at home or outside. However, even now, my method to come up with ideas for my films is ideally to withdraw to a pleasant place to relax: it could be a field at the edge of a forest, a beach, or even my desk in my studio, where I start thinking, fantasizing, scribbling down my ideas in the notebook I always carry with me. On these occasions, I never sketch or draw; the ideas popping up are still abstract, and besides, writing down story imagery goes much faster than actually sketching it.

Even in those early days in Moscow, the drawings I made were not much like the usual kid drawings; I never drew the house with the chimney and smoke coming out of it; or the cow in the field with the sun and clouds in the sky. Instead, I would draw characters with big noses in often funny situations, like someone stumbling over an insect; or a long-legged rider on a short-legged horse; or dogs waiting in line for an available tree. In fact, I always drew 'stories'.

An early drawing, done when I was about 10 years old.

I remember that once, when I drew a vase with flowers instead of a funny cartoon as a birthday drawing for my grandmother, both my grandmother and my mother asked me if something was wrong. Had my grandmother said something offensive? Was I in a bad mood?

Although my sister and I did a lot of drawing, which they certainly encouraged, my parents had a hard time judging the quality of our output and the artwork of others we liked. When, for example, some issues of the newly created Tintin magazine arrived in the late 40s, my mother deemed the calibre of the text very low (she was quite right about that, of course), and because she didn't share our enthusiasm for the pictures, the subscription of the magazine was cancelled. Her view of the upcoming art of the comics was quite common amongst European intellectuals; storytelling through pictures was not considered literature nor part of the visual arts, and thus denounced.

For people who don't value the quality of the artwork, balloon texts don't contribute to the attraction of the comics.

The toll the Russians had paid to help win the war had left the country very poor. But despite all the deprivation they suffered, the Soviets dedicated a lot of their limited resources to the upbringing of their young.

I vividly remember visits to puppet theatre shows and musicals specially created for children. We had Russian dance lessons from Ivan Ivanovich and singing lessons from Nicolai Nicolaievich (my spelling might be wrong, but those were their real names). We also went to concerts, heard the rumbling voices and beautiful harmonies of the Don Cossack choir and at home, my parents had an extensive collection of records of Russian songs, some of which I later used as soundtracks in my films.

The only films we ever saw during that time (and I was tremendously impressed by them) were shown at the American Embassy: a Western in which kids went after horse thieves and a comedy with two American sailors transported to Roman times. At a certain point in the story, they hid in large jars on top of the steps of a temple and misled the Roman soldiers chasing them, after which the jars tipped over and rolled down the steps. We also saw a Russian documentary about wildlife, including animals fleeing from forest fires, with an amazing underwater scene of a fight between a beaver and a pike. Although I tried, I have never been able to track down any of these films.

When we moved back to the Netherlands in 1950, my parents decided to send their three children to the Montessori school in Rotterdam. The Montessori system was a non-authoritarian kind of education which suited us well after the years of private lessons given by our mother. Holland already prided itself on Montessori schools in four of its big cities, not only for primary schooling but also for further education, leading up to university levels. It was a fairly new system in those days, and Marietje de Haan, the director of the Rotterdam school we went to, had been taught by Maria Montessori herself.

My brother Robs, my sister Annemargreet and me, back in Holland in the early 50s.

Going to a real school with lots of kids was a new and startling experience for me. Having been in the company of so few people for so long, my social skills were rather lacking, but, because of my funny drawings, I quickly made friends. Curiously, since the harbour city of Rotterdam had a large socialist establishment, our background of having lived in Russia, appeared to be a popular asset.

I was a slow pupil, and the grammar school curriculum was very demanding; I was taught Latin, Greek, English, French, German, and Dutch literature, plus all the science subjects—not easy for a kid whose main interest was drawing cartoons. I repeated quite a few classes, but in the end, learning to speak and write four languages proved very beneficial for my international animation career. My English was quite adequate when I moved to London in the 60s; my French was passable when I worked at the French animation department of the National Film Board in Montreal in the 70s; and in the 90s, when I became an animation professor at the University of Kassel in Germany, my German was good enough to help my students with their projects.

My primary Montessori class. I'm sitting on the far left.

I also learned to appreciate the richness of knowing various languages. I always felt that people who sometimes out of fear of the unknown or distrust, shied away from the language of other cultures were missing out on so much of what that culture was about. I knew quite a few English Canadians who, although living in the predominantly French-speaking city of Montreal, hardly spoke any French. When I read a Dutch book or when I'm on the phone with friends in Holland, talking about the typical and often hilarious ways of expression of the Dutch, I always feel sorry that I can't share this pleasure with the French or English-speaking people in the country where I live.

God, creating Europe, pondering over cultural peculiarities

My language cartoon inspired by a fellow cartoonist.

Frequently, when I had difficulties with certain subjects at school, my mother, ever a great teacher, would step in and help out. She also lent a hand to many of our struggling schoolmates, and our house often became a welcome refuge for friends who had difficulties at home.

With our new friends, we discovered the thrills the Dutch outdoors offered to kids: *ijsje piepen* (running and sliding fast over the thin ice of the canals and lakes surrounding Rotterdam, trying to get to the other side without breaking through, often not without danger) and *slootje springen* (a short run over soggy grassland then trying to jump over canals of various widths which crisscrossed the polders around our home, also not without danger).

Since the streets of the suburb where we lived were relatively quiet in the 50s, we played all kinds of street games—hopscotch, jumping ropes, marbles, even soccer (I once kicked the ball through our neighbour's window, a rather regular occurrence in Holland, frequently colourfully described in Dutch children's books).

As kids we also took up swimming, sailing, and skating, typical sports for a country that not so long ago in history, was mostly submerged in water. After spending most of my life in foreign countries, I still get excited when, on a cold winter's day in Holland, I approach a dike looming up in the countryside, behind which I see a line up of speed-skaters moving at great speed with their elegant long slow strokes.

During the summer vacations, my parents, who had learned to appreciate the popular German *Freie Körper Kultur* (free body culture) in the thirties in Berlin, took us often to nudist camping sites which slowly emerged in various countries in Europe.

The most beautiful camping I remember is from the 50s, at Île-du-Levant, a French nudist island which, surrounded by lovely beaches, offered great swimming and snorkelling in the Mediterranean Sea full of colourful fish, sea urchins and octopuses. The island also organized the yearly election of Miss Île-du-Levant, a line-up of young naked ladies, the winner of which was customarily invited to spend the evening on one of the many luxurious yachts which cluttered the island. It was an event which nowadays certainly would be frowned upon.

"Harry always takes an hour or so to make absolutely sure they're bathing in the nude before he reports them to the police."

Giles cartoon.

The very first summer we settled in Rotterdam, my grandfather moved in with us, my grandmother having died the year before. My mother didn't get along with him too well, as he was quite demanding. But I fondly remember that in the evenings, my sister and I would sit on his lap while he read to us the instalments of the popular comic strip Tom Poes, beautifully written and illustrated by Marten Toonder. The text accompanying the illustrations didn't appear in balloons but was placed beneath the panels, allowing for better and more elaborate writing.

Nu, Tom Poes kwam heelhuids in de sloep beneden en toen die in het water lag, sprong Wal Rus naast hem en greep de riemen. 'We moeten maken dat we wegkomen,' zei hij. 'Anders worden we meegesleept als het schip zinkt.' En hij begon te roeien zo hard hij kon. Op hetzelfde ogenblik stak de wind op en blies de mist even vlug weer weg als hij gekomen was. 'Het is toch jammer van de Albatros,' zei Wal Rus. 'Ze was wel oud, maar toch was ik aan haar gehecht, meneer. Het spijt me, dat ik haar hier in de Poolzee achter moet laten. Bah! Foei! Die overgehaalde ijsbergen bederven mijn humeur. Heb je trouwens in de gaten, dat er storm op til is? We kunnen het nog koud krijgen in dit bootje.' Wal Rus had gelijk. De wind begon op te steken, de zee werd met de minuut onrustiger en er begon een ijskoude regen, vermengd met sneeuw, te vallen...

Martin Toonder's Tom Poes *comic strip.*

Although I offered my services to the Toonder Studios later in life (they also had a small animation department) I never worked for them, but I always maintained a keen interest in the beautiful prose and design style of the work of its founder.

Holland in the 50s and early 60s was very interested in the French culture. There were many French cafés, dark places, netting hanging from the ceilings and candles on the tables where customers would smoke Gauloises, drink wine and listen to French chansons—Charles Trenet, Juliette Gréco, Georges Brassens, Jacques Brel, Léo Ferré, Guy Béart, Yves Montand, Gilbert Bécaud, and Barbara. We played their records over and over again, humming along as French was not an easy language for the Dutch.

My mother had taught me the basics of playing the guitar, and I had learned many of the beautiful French songs by heart. I was not a very good player, nor did I have a strong singing voice, but at least my efforts won the heart of one young woman who thought my feeble efforts were cute. Then the British invasion came about—first Skiffle, then the Beatles and the Stones and all the other exciting sounds which made our bodies move, and the more poetic French approach to music slowly disappeared from the Dutch musical landscape.

The French were also good at my main interest, cartoons. I loved the elegance of Sempé; 'Les Amoureux' of Peynet; Chaval; Siné and the vulgar fun of Dubout (who was also known for his posters for Marcel Pagnol).

Dubout's poster for Fanny.

Growing up, I never considered any other future occupation than cartooning. I realized that I wasn't made for an academic career, and I wasn't technical (although I had a flair for original, often 'funny' solutions to fix small problems, making things work with the help of strings, elastics and paperclips), but I appreciated humorous situations (from my father's side) and creative thinking (from my mother's side).

Although they never said so, I'm sure my parents were worried about my future. But they also understood that for me to succeed in life, I had to pursue my talents for cartoon drawing, so they always supported my choice in that direction, even without being able to fully appreciate the outcome of my work.

When I was about nineteen, I gathered all my courage and set out to see if I could sell my one-panel cartoons. I took a bus to Paris, bought all the magazines sporting cartoons at a newspaper stand, and wrote down the names and addresses of the publishers located in Paris. I then went to the various addresses and, curiously enough, was often invited in to show my drawings. The editors were usually nice and friendly. They spent time looking at my work, and some even asked me to leave my cartoons behind for consideration, but in the end, I never sold any of them.

Shortly after my Paris adventure, I took the ferry to England and repeated my efforts to sell my cartoons to London magazine publishers. Again, I was welcomed in at most places just by knocking on their doors, but in the end, I was not able to get any of my cartoons published.

Not very long after these excursions I found out about a Dutch cartoonist, Ton Smits, who wasn't very well known in Holland but had quite a few of his cartoons published in the New Yorker. When I phoned Ton, he was very friendly and told me he lived with his mother in a small town in the southern part of our country and that he would pick me up at the town's station in his pink little DAF, a locally manufactured car which the Dutch called 'an old lady' car.

I still remember that when I set out to meet Ton Smits, my mother told me to 'be careful,' which was a puzzling remark to me. Much later, I understood that she wanted to warn me that Ton probably was gay and that I, being a kind of amenable young man (I was a late bloomer, had not brought any girlfriends home yet) might be drawn to this inclination.

I guess this reservation of my mother's went way back to my childhood in Moscow. Like any young boy I played with toy cars and built structures from wooden blocks. But I had also asked for a doll with flexible joints for my eighth birthday and enjoyed sewing colourful dresses for it. Also, my sister and I shared a toy oven in which we pretended to cook pastries.

Although it never occurred to me to tell my parents, I was always interested in the male body, not as a sexual object, but as a form of beauty. As a teenager I felt a bit like a shrimp myself, so next to my appreciation of the aesthetics, there was also some jealousy involved. My interest in the shape of male bodies never turned into any sexual desire, though, and in the end, I didn't think my own physique was so bad.

My mother didn't have to be worried. Ton, a very kind man, appeared to have no interest in my body. He was not only a good cartoonist but also a very interesting painter; his colourful art was all over the walls of his house, including the bedrooms, bathroom, and toilet. When Ton passed away in 1981, his wife and a group of close friends turned his house into a small museum.

When I asked Ton how he had managed to get his cartoons into such a prestigious magazine as The New Yorker, he told me that by just sending his cartoons over and over again to the editors, he had established some kind of familiarity and had perhaps created the impression that he was a well-known cartoonist. I'm sure the New Yorker also recognized his talent; his cartoons were really funny.

Ton Smits' cartoon.

By this time, I was really starting to appreciate not only cartoons but also styles of drawing by various artists, both inside and outside of Holland.

My favourite Dutch artists were Marten Toonder, famous for his *Tom Poes* comic strip, beautifully drawn and well written; Jo Spier, who drew very delicate black and white illustrations; Hans Kresse, whose graphic strip *Eric the Norman* featured heroic adventurers, men with great bodies in Nordic landscapes; And Yrrah, an illustrator of morbid cartoons.

From Belgium and France, I enjoyed *Tintin* by Hergé, the originator of the 'clear line'; Morris's *Lucky Luke,* always with a wink to true stories from the Wild West; and the refined humour in the drawings of Sempé.

Sempé.

From England, I admired E.H. Shepard and his lovely illustrations for *Winnie the Pooh* and *The Wind in the Willows*; the strong graphic drawings by Ronald Searle; Thelwell's very British horsing around cartoons; and Giles' great semi-political cartoons for the *Daily Express.*

The many American artists who stood out for me were George Herriman, with his strong style and crazy ideas of *Krazy Kat*; Otto Soglow and the simple wit of *The Little King*; Jules Pfeiffer's poetic ideas and style; Al Capp, who, with *Lil Abner,* had created what I felt was something very American; Rudolph Dirks whose *The Katzenjammer Kids* I had already discovered as a child; and Saul Steinberg, an inspiration for many of us, including the earlier mentioned Ton Smits.

E.H. Shepard, Winnie the Pooh.

In the early 60s, army service in

George Herriman, Krazy Kat.

Holland was compulsory and for many young men like me who wanted to embark on the journey of life, we were stuck for at least one and a half years in what many considered an outdated regimented system.

The first six months of my service was physically tough: running, jumping, carrying your mates on your back, all in full battle gear. Not pleasant, but at least we got in good shape. And I learned to shoot the newly acquired Israeli Uzi. I can't say I enjoyed shooting guns, and I wasn't very good at hitting targets, but our main occupation with the Uzi wasn't so much using the weapon but taking it apart, cleaning it and putting it back together. Maybe an interesting pursuit if you were a mechanic, less interesting if you were an aspiring cartoonist.

There was a scary moment during this time in which I might have had to make use of my Uzi. The colony of Dutch New Guinea was fighting for its independence and Dutch soldiers were asked to volunteer to suppress the rebellion. Fortunately, there were enough volunteers to comply with the numbers needed for this futile enterprise, but there was a fear, however short-lived, that soldiers might be ordered to go over and fight the local Papuans. Particularly, the notion that the Papuans were reputed to be cannibals and head-hunters didn't really appeal to me.

After six months of being drilled into shape, a year of complete

The French Revolution created a great boom in the trade relationship between France and the headhunters of New Guinea.

boredom followed. Every morning my regiment had to get up at 5 a.m., then, after breakfast, we had to wait for the train at 8 a.m., to get us to the next village. There, for the rest of the day, we did very simple and seemingly useless administrative work, such as making sure the Dutch army had enough buttons to stitch onto their uniforms or that the number of tanks available corresponded with the numbers on our lists.

Fortunately, there was an art school in Utrecht, the city where I served, which gave evening classes at the Graphic Arts department. Although I was often quite tired after a very long day of doing nothing much, at night at least I could work on what I assumed would probably be useful for my future, learning about lettering, printing, photography, and poster design. My cartoon style wasn't really appreciated, though; Holland didn't have a tradition in funny drawings.

After my military service, I had a hard time finding work. While finishing the last two years of my evening classes at the art school, during the day I was much by myself, sitting in a small, rented room in the suburbs of Utrecht, working on cartoon drawings nobody wanted. I remember it as the most depressing time of my life. *I like it heavy* and *Puffball* are two cartoons from

"I like it heavy, but I can't get up."
A cartoon inspired by the equipment I had to deal with when serving in the army.

that period which, as nobody wanted them, were never published.

Then one day, just by chance, I read an article in a newspaper about Cine Cartoon Center, an animation studio in Hilversum, a town not far from Amsterdam. Its director, the American animator Jim Hiltz, was interviewed about the upcoming commercial television in the Netherlands and next to his photograph the paper showed some pictures of his studio work.

Although I didn't know anything about animation, it sounded very

"Puffball!!!"

exciting and I made an appointment with Jim to visit the studio, secretly hoping that he might need someone like me. It was a lucky stroke; Jim liked my drawing style and humour and hired me on the spot.

Thus, in the spring of 1964, I started my animation career.

Discovering the Art of Animation

The Cine Cartoon Center team consisted of Jim Hiltz and one other animator, the Dutchman Ronald Bijlsma. Downstairs, at the stop-motion and puppet studio, worked Co Hoedeman who, like Ronald, became a good friend.

Jim Hiltz was a great draughtsman and an animator of the UPA tradition: expressive simple limited animation, the opposite of the elaborate Disney style. When I told him that I had no idea how to animate he just gave me a few hints about balance, weight and anticipation, provided me with an animation disk, gave me a pile of punched animation paper and told me to go ahead and try out some movements.

After completing my first walking cycle I was directed to the camera department downstairs where CineCentrum (the mother company) had installed an Oxberry animation camera-stand, attended by a cameraman who would shoot my line-test on 35mm B&W High-Contrast. The material would be developed the same day at the lab in the building next door, which was also part of the CineCentrum complex.

I learned fast, and soon after, I wrote, designed, and animated my first assignment– a ten second commercial for an industrial glue which had just come on the market. My little film was never shown on Dutch TV; ten seconds appeared to be too short for distribution according to the newly devised Dutch commercial television directory.

However, my glue-commercial drew the attention of an animation festival in France, which had been founded a few years before, and in 1965 I accompanied my ten second film to my first Annecy festival. Many visits followed, but at the time I had no idea which turn my life would take.

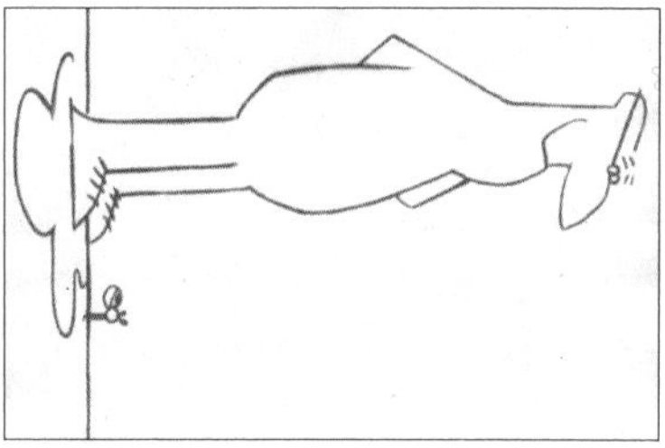

My 10-second glue commercial.

The 1965 Annecy festival was a great eye opener; it was still a relatively small festival, located at the border of a beautiful lake with a view of the Alps. All the great artists of the 'independent animated shorts' were either present or had sent their films to the festival.

There was a great variety of styles and techniques: pixelation, cut-outs and puppet animation by the East European masters, Jan Svankmajer, Jiri Trinka, Bratislav Pojar, Jan Leniça; experimental work by the Canadian Norman McLaren and the Russian-French-American couple Alexeieff-Parker; painterly animation from Jean-François Laguionie of France (who won the Grand Prix that year); crazy imagery from Yoji Kuri; witty cartoons out of England by George Dunning and Bob Godfrey; and colourful shorts from the Americans John Hubley, Jimmy Marukami, and Fred Wolff. It was a truly fascinating overview of what the art of animation was about.

My first bow from Annecy's balcony, presenting one of my earlier films.

Meanwhile, Cine Cartoon Center became involved in animating a series based on the songs of an emerging British pop-group called The Beatles. The series was produced by TV Cartoons in London and Jim Hiltz invited two other experienced animators from abroad to work with him on the series at our studio in Holland. Since the Beatles were very productive, writing one song after another, the series had to be animated at great speed and the exhausted animators were often seen late at night bent over their animation desks, trying to cut corners. Ronald and I were fortunately exempt and quietly continued to work at our commercials.

A Jim Hiltz cartoon about the necessity of budget-saving corner cutting during the work on the Beatles TV series.

The model sheet I drew of Heinz Edelmann's character design when working on the Yellow Submarine.

George Dunning, the artistic director of the Beatles series, visited Cine Cartoon Centre a couple of times and at a certain point stopped by and looked at my work. He apparently liked what I did and told me that if I ever wanted to come to London, I would be welcome at his studio.

In 1966, our animation department at Cine Cartoon Center collapsed. Jim had gone back to the US, and since most Dutch advertising agencies turned to the more experienced English studios for their commercials, there was very little work for Ronald and myself, the two remaining animators. Remembering George Dunning's standing invitation, I made an appointment with him and travelled to his studio in London. It was good timing, as TV Cartoons had just embarked on a new project, an animated feature film.

After the success of the Beatles series and based on the popularity of the Beatles themselves, the American production studio United Artists proposed to TVC to make an animated 90-minute film featuring the Beatles' last album, *Sgt. Pepper's Lonely Hearts Club Band*. *The Yellow Submarine*, the song John and Paul had written for Ringo, became the film's title.

I started in the very early days of the production. There was no script, no character design, just a contract with the American companies United

Artists and King Features to make an animated feature based on Sgt. Pepper's Lonely Hearts Club Band.

Since there were some rumours that the band might break up, which gave rise to the fear that the interest in a film based on the Beatles would fade, the project had to be made in the shortest possible time—in no more than eleven months (Disney generally needed around four to five years for its feature productions). The budget, I remember, was one million dollars, not a very large amount for an animated feature, even for that time. But then, the United Artists production studio had a rather low-cost cartoon in mind, more or less made in the style of the Beatles series they had produced before.

Fortunately, the film's director, the Canadian George Dunning, a visionary and great artist who had been schooled at the National Film Board of Canada by Norman McLaren, had other ideas about what the film should be like. While a small bunch of us started out suggesting ideas, sketching storyboards, inspired by the Sgt. Pepper songs, George Dunning began an intensive search for the designer of the film. I still remember the day that we all flocked to George's office where he showed us the artwork of Heinz Edelmann, a Czech-German illustrator. Heinz appeared not only to be able to beautifully capture the spirit of the songs in his designs, but he also was an important force behind the many visual ideas that were scattered throughout the film.

Still, there was no script and TVC, United Artists, Brian Epstein, and even the Beatles themselves, all checked out a variety of writers who could tackle the difficult task of squeezing a series of very different unrelated songs into a somewhat coherent screenplay.

At an early stage of the production, the American animator Jimmy Marukami, who often dropped into the studio when he was around, assembled a small group of us. During a day-long brainstorming session, while pinning roughly drawn pictures of songs and possible action on the wall, he proceeded to map out some kind of story for the film. Based on this first attempt, a writer named Lee Minoff, together with the film's designer Heinz Edelmann and the two unit directors assisted by their wives wrote a more elaborate basic outline.

In the end, when the first fifteen minutes of the film were already animated, the American writer Erich Segal, then an assistant professor at Yale (who had not yet written his famous novel *Love Story*), was brought in, mainly to write the dialogues. A Liverpool friend of the Beatles, the poet Roger McCough, was hired to make it sound more British.

Although it was a very chaotic production with pressure from the American producers for shortcuts and staunch resistance from TVC to maintain the high standards of George Dunning's vision, our small team of 25 animators quietly set out to animate the 90-minute film. All in all, only about 200 people were on the *Yellow Submarine* staff, a tiny group of people compared to the numbers on later animated feature productions.

I remember the strong impression Paul McCartney made on me when he came by early in the production to see what we were doing. He had been an iconic image for so long that it really struck me meeting the handsome young man in real life. After showing him some of our storyboards, the studio manager brought Paul to the ink and paint department, a room full of young women screaming their heads off at the sight of him.

The Beatles themselves were hardly involved in the production. It was the period in the band's existence when they were involved with the spiritual leader, the Maharishi Yogi, and wanted to spend time with him in India. Therefore, an animated film in which they would be represented by drawn characters was an easy way out of the commitment they had with United Artists. After *A Hard Day's Night* and *Help* they apparently signed up for a third film with that company. Now, all they had to do was appear briefly at the very end of the film to fulfil their contract.

The 60s in London was a very memorable time. I was 27 years old, enjoying the free spirit atmosphere of a city where clearly 'the times-were-a-changing'. The TVC studios were in the Soho district in the centre of London, and when I would emerge from the Tube station on my way to work, I would step into an area where the streets, parks and pubs were crowded with young people dressed in wild colours, mixed in with the typical British office workers in their dark striped suits and bowlers. Nearby was the vibrant Carnaby Street and lively Portobello Road market;

the Rolling Stones were getting popular; the musical *Hair* opened, and in October of that year, I married Fieke, my Dutch love who came to live with me in England.

☆ ☆ ☆

My time in the UK lasted only as long as the duration of the production of the Yellow Submarine, and somewhat reluctantly we returned to Holland, not knowing what to do next. After vainly exploring the options to work as a commercial animator, I eventually succeeded in getting a subsidy to make my first independent animated short, called *The Story of Little Yoghurt.* Since we had very little money and no place to live, we decided to fill up our little Fiat with punched animation paper and head for Spain, where the cost of living was much cheaper than in the Netherlands.

We found a small apartment in Vinaroz, a town at the Mediterranean, halfway between Barcelona and Valencia, and I settled down to work.

Storyboard for The Killing of an Egg.

We had a lovely time; we explored our new environment, swam in the sea, and even went to our first (and last) bullfight in the local arena. Fieke, pregnant with our first child, studied the Spanish language and local cuisine while I happily worked on my six-minute Little Yogurt film.

It was a very productive time in my life. While finishing the animation for *The Story of Little Yoghurt,* I also made storyboards for a few more ideas I came up with. One called *The Killing of an Egg,* eventually made into an animated film six years after its conception, became one of my best-known films.

In Vinaroz, I also wrote and designed a comic strip called Jonas, plus I set up a series of small books with slightly off-beat illustrated stories for children, *The Fiddle Fumble Stories* (which would be published many years later).

Although there was recurring interest over the years, Jonas has never been in print. I have always been fortunate that most of the ideas for stories and films I really believed in eventually saw the light, so I still have hope for *Jonas.*

Three panels of my comic strip, Jonas. The leader of a group of nomads wandering through the desert is swallowed by a snake. The group decides to adjust to the new situation by following the example of their leader (who communicates with them through icons in his speech balloons) and look for suitable large animals for accommodation. Jonas, of course, ends up in a whale.

In the fall of 1969 Fieke and I moved back to the Netherlands. With the little money we had left from the production, we were able to rent a small cabin in the woods in the east of the country and in November our daughter Anouk was born.

During my work on the *Yellow Submarine,* I had many discussions with its director George Dunning, about where to go next. George had been trained at the National Film Board of Canada and spoke highly of this institution, which allowed filmmakers from both inside and outside of Canada to make their personal projects.

Once I realized that there wasn't really a future for me making personal animated shorts in Holland, I decided to approach the National Film Board of Canada in Montreal. Although I received friendly answers to my letters, the Film Board didn't offer to invite me over but told me that if I were in Montreal, I should certainly drop in to discuss projects which might be of interest.

Through animation friends in London, I heard of Gerald Potterton, an English animation director who had worked at the National Film Board but, after a few years of making shorts, had successfully started his own animation studio in Montreal. He was setting up an animated feature called *Tiki-Tiki* and was looking for animators. (Curiously, only later in the production of *Tiki-Tiki,* I realized that the live footage mixed with the animation was old material from Russia, telling the story of a doctor who was stuck in the jungle with a bunch of monkeys. The original movie was made from a kid's theatre show I had seen in Moscow as a child called *Doktor Aybolit*—Doctor-ouch-it-hurts.)

I applied for the job to animate on *Tiki-Tiki,* and Gerry flew me over. May 1970 was the first time I set foot on North American soil.

MEETING THE CANADIANS

After arriving in Montreal, I made an appointment with Bob Verrall, the head of the English Animation department at the National Film Board, the person George Dunning had referred me to, and showed him many of my ideas for animated shorts. He was very nice to me but did not really appear interested.

Later, when I discovered the many very funny films produced by the English animation program like *What on Earth, Hot Stuff* and many more, I realized that what made these films so good was not only the great animation but also the witty dialogues. I found out that, historically,

English-speaking countries, more than other cultures, have a great fondness for quality dialogue in films.

My English was rather feeble in those early days, and the storyboards I presented to Bob Verrall had no dialogue in them, just captions explaining the storyboard panels. Bob might not have been very impressed by my ideas, of course, but the lack of good dialogue probably didn't help.

Fortunately for me, there was also the French Animation department at the National Film Board. Canada is a bicultural country, and therefore, all federal institutions, including the National Film Board, have both English and French programs. Animators who were not from English-speaking countries and who used a more visual narrative to express themselves were usually more welcome on the French side. As French was only understood by a minority in North America, the distribution of films in which the French language was spoken was very limited.

René Jodoin, the head of the French Animation department, liked my work. Ecology was already a subject of importance in the 70s, so he chose my idea, Le Bleu Perdu, as my first Film Board project. The story is about a boy who is bothered by the accumulation of pollution in the air and decides to go up to the heavens to find out what causes it and how it can be stopped.

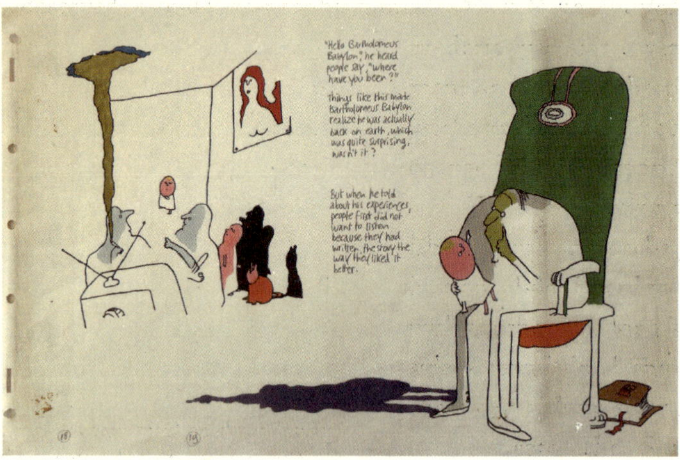

Storyboard page for Le Bleu Perdu.

What I found interesting was that, at the time, the French and English animation departments were not only on different floors and separated by long corridors but were also not very keen on contact. It almost seemed that they were trying to protect their own cultural identity by avoiding each other. When, for instance, I went upstairs to see people on the English side, some of whom I had met during the production of the *Yellow Submarine* in London, to ask about what kind of cels and paint were available in Montreal, my French-Canadian producers made it clear that we didn't need their advice and they would rather do the research themselves.

Now, having arrived in the 21st century in a more globalized world, the English and French departments at the National Film Board are very close. The difference in identity is, nonetheless, still apparent through the choice of filmmakers and projects on both sides.

One aspect of having a project secured at the National Film Board in the early 70s was that I needed a visa to extend my stay in Canada and to allow my young family to come over.

I visited the immigration office in Montreal and when the agent in charge asked me for how long I needed my visa, I explained that I had a National Film Board contract and would need at least a year to make my film. He then leaned over and said that, though he wasn't officially allowed to tell me, why not just immigrate to Canada? When he assured me that there were no consequences like losing my Dutch passport, I readily complied, and five minutes later I had the status of 'landed immigrant' in Canada, which meant that if I wanted, I could stay in Canada the rest of my life without having to apply for visas ever again.

In October that year, Fieke and our one-year-old Anouk came over (while little Kaj was in the making) and we found a small convenient apartment not far from the National Film Board offices, at cycling distance in summer, and walking distance in winter.

Le Bleu Perdu was a bit of a struggle, and although it came out well in the end, I proposed a much simpler idea for my next project, a two-minute film called Air. Again, its subject was pollution. In this case the drama was focused on a horizontal line that divided the screen in two. The line

Cinéfiche / AIR! (1972) | Version 214144 / Dir. Paul Driessen | © National Film Board of Canada

The poster for Air, *a 2-minute short made at the French Animation department at the NFB.*

represented a variety of items: land surface with suffocating plants on top; water surface with suffocating fish below; a wire on which a suffocating bird perched; and land again in which a suffocating man tried to hide by digging a hole. The hole turned into an air bubble, which, as the man inside was gasping for breath, grew smaller and smaller until it entirely disappeared.

Air was my first film in a long chain of projects wherein I experimented with a way of storytelling which, as I later learned, was coined 'Narrative Space.' Scholars like the Portuguese filmmaker and journalist Pedro Serrazina and the Ukrainian graduate student Alina Milkina described in their dissertations that, unlike linear storytelling (showing characters going through a slice of their lives from A to B) in narrative space we apply all the options open to the art of filmmaking: image, colour, movement, icons and symbols, dimensions, framing and sound, which includes music and voices. Throughout this book, I will give examples of my use of narrative space. This approach to storytelling shows up in almost all of my films.

The audience, when faced by the line in Air, which split the screen in two, had no idea what it represented, until I introduced the various creatures which then established its meaning and made it part of their particular environments. There was only heavy breathing on the soundtrack. The whole film was drawn on slightly transparent grainy old newsprint, which, shot frame by frame, gave the impression of moving fog particles. I was only able to obtain 300 sheets of old newsprint from the Film Board's storage, so

Flowers, fish, birds, and humans all gasp for air and ultimately succumb to pollution.

my animation was limited to just 300 drawings, which, for an animated film of that length, is not a lot.

Working at the French Animation unit was very enjoyable. It was a fairly young department; the French production was only established after the National Film Board moved its headquarters from Ottawa, the Canadian capital situated in the province of Ontario, to Montreal in the province of Québec.

Photo: Nico Crama

Picnic with Canadian filmmakers at the 'mountain,' Mont Royal, in Montreal.

Most of the animators working at the French Animation were about my age. Some were on staff, and others were freelancers like me. Also, my Dutch friend Co Hoedeman, who had emigrated to Canada a few years before me, had moved from the National

Film Board's Documentary unit to the French Animation.

Our department experimented with all sorts of techniques: drawn, painted, pixilated, puppet and object animation, cut-outs, scratch-on-film, and a procedure we would now call mixed media, which in the early 70s was primarily a handcrafted art. It wasn't all high-quality filmmaking, but the atmosphere was lively, and people often came up with maybe somewhat rudimentary but creative ideas.

As well as animators from France (whom we called the French-French), our department also attracted animators from other countries: the American Caroline Leaf, famous for her sand animation and films painted on glass, was invited to the National Film Board in '72, as was her compatriot Lynn Smith, an expert of various under-the-camera techniques, and the well-known Czech animator Břetislav Pojar visited our studio during that time and animated his film Balablok, using squares and triangles cut out from paper.

The French Animation also became known for its parties, which, compared to the standing-drinking-talking parties in the English Animation, were pretty wild. I still vividly remember a full bathtub sitting in the room amongst the dancing crowd, a lot of splashing going on inside! And when 'streaking' became popular, that too was included in our parties as part of the fun.

My new friends introduced us to the French-Canadian culture, experimental theatre and dance, and the music scene. As a European, I had never heard any of the great French-Canadian singers: Felix Leclerc, Pauline Julien, Gilles Vigneault, Robert Charlebois and many more—a delightful surprise!

Fieke and I discovered the Canadian outdoors, the vastness of the land, its forests, and lakes. In the spring of 1972, my adventurous father-in-law came over for a visit and proposed that we should go on a trip to explore the Canadian wilderness. We drove up to Parc de la Vérendrye, one of the enormous national parks in the North of Quebec, rented a tent and a couple of canoes and took off. We got lost in the woods, capsized in the rapids, heard the haunting cry of the loon, met moose and a bear scouring for food outside our tent (we were lucky that the beast didn't consider us as food), and after four days of adventure, we returned exhausted, hungry and with torn clothes (and my father-in-law slightly bloodied). At the reception space of the park, there was a warm fire and a meal waiting for us.

We noticed that a very well-equipped group of professional looking outdoorsmen shared a table next to us and when we inquired who they were it appeared to be Sir Edmund Hillary (the one who had conquered the Mount Everest) and his team. They were also setting out on a canoe trip but were clearly better prepared.

Nonetheless, the experience had warmed us to the attractions of the great outdoors, and we continued walking in the woods and canoeing and swimming in the lakes. In the early 70s, the Canadian forests didn't have many trails for hikers. In Europe, we were used to forests full of small crisscrossing roads, created over centuries of communicating traffic between villages and towns. The Canadian woods, on the other hand, were too big and the land too sparsely populated to make the creation of walking paths viable. Only in later years, especially when cross-country skiing became popular, did the government start cutting trails for leisure activities.

January 1971,
in the woods outside Montreal.

In the following winters, I often took off with friends cross-country skiing in the woods around Montreal, a sport perfect as an outdoor winter activity in Québec. Although quite a few hills are high enough for downhill skiing, there are few big mountains in Québec, so most of the ski slopes are rather short. Waiting in long line-ups for ski lifts only to have a short descent in often very cold temperatures was never my cup of tea.

Cross-country skiing, on the other hand, on the many trails over the abundance of beautiful hills one- or two-hour drive from the city, far from the populated ski slopes, was hard physical work but immensely satisfying. Alone or with a small group of friends, enjoying the beauty of the landscape, you were kept warm by the constant effort of climbing the hills or trying to keep your balance when going down. Crashing into trees or missing bends and trying to get back up from being upside down in the deep snow next to the trail was another part of the sport which kept you warm.

The year I arrived in Montreal, 1970, was also the year that the Front de Liberation du Québec (FLQ) came back into the news. The FLQ was a separatist terrorist organization established in the 60s which wanted the province of Québec to separate from the rest of Canada. In October '70, the FLQ kidnapped James Cross, the British trade commissioner in Montreal, and abducted and later killed Pierre Laporte, the labour minister and vice-premier of Québec.

During the fall of that year, walking in the forests was not without danger. The police hadn't found the terrorist cells yet who had killed Laporte and held the British trade commissioner captive, and they suspected that they might be hiding in the woods around the city. Eventually, they were caught, some in a hide-out in the city, others in a farmhouse outside Montreal.

In '73, my marriage collapsed, and Fieke and our two little kids went back to Holland. Those were sad days, and I often felt depressed and lonely, but friends and work kept me going. My films started winning prizes, and I was being sent to festivals to represent them. Winning awards for freelance animators like me was important, not so much for the honour but rather to get noticed by the institutions that we needed to sponsor our future films.

When my project, *David,* was rejected by the National Film Board, I decided to ask for a subsidy in the Netherlands. A new relationship in Canada hadn't worked out, I missed my children, whom I hadn't seen for quite a long time, and I was ready for a new adventure.

So, when the Dutch accepted my proposal for *David,* I was happy to return to the Netherlands, and in the spring of 1976, I flew back to Amsterdam.

THE NOMAD LIFE OF A DUAL CITIZEN

When I moved back to Holland in '76 and found myself a small apartment close to the Scheveningen beach, next to the city of The Hague, it happened to be one of the most beautiful worldwide summers ever.

That year, the Dutch had opened up long stretches of nudist beaches, a ten-minute bike ride from my place, and while working on *David* in the mornings and evenings, I spent many an afternoon on the beach, swimming, jogging, playing volleyball, but always bringing a notebook with me, jotting down ideas, writing stories for future projects.

A curious thing worth mentioning about the more than one-kilometer-long nudist beach was that all along that stretch, the municipality had erected a two-meter high wooden wall close to the side of the dunes, which provided a shield for people who preferred to go for a stroll on the beach

"Far enough, Adonis."

Giles cartoon about nudists.

without seeing naked people and being bothered by uncovered genitals. Each winter, a time when the fun of taking off your clothes was less compelling, the wall would be taken down. and each spring, it would be put back up. This procedure lasted quite a few years until the people in charge realized that nobody ever walked behind the partition, so they dropped the ideology behind it. and the wall was never seen again.

Photo: Fieke Sutorius

Anouk and Kaj's big smiles.

Fieke and our children Anouk and Kaj had left Canada in '73 so I hadn't seen my kids in about three years. It was actually quite a surprise to see them grown much taller with charming toothy smiles.

☆ ☆ ☆

David was another one of my films, which is typical of my narrative space experiments. The film was about a character, David, whom I didn't have to animate for he was so small that you couldn't see him. However, David had a strong voice with which he explained his ordeal. and at certain moments, he told us where he was situated on screen by giving some clues.

David showing his 'long hair' to indicate where he is situated on screen.

Because David was so little, the world he lived in was a dangerous place for him; either people around him might step on him because they didn't see him, or certain individuals (Goliath, a bird of prey 'with sharp eyes') were out to get him.

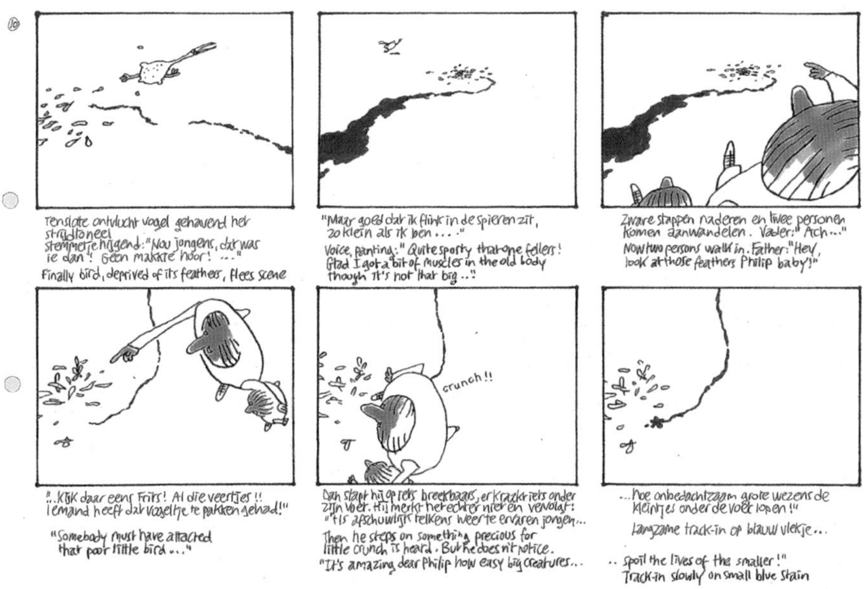

Storyboard page for David.

Photo: Nico Crama

Working on David *in my small studio in The Hague.*

The larger creatures who put his life in danger had to appear on screen, of course, but all in all there wasn't much animation to be done. Making your audience look at an empty screen most of the time was kind of an animator's dream; I finished the film way before the date I had booked for my flight to return to Canada.

Meanwhile, I had befriended the Dutch producer, Nico Crama, who lived in the neighbourhood. Nico was one of the most prominent independent producers of animated shorts in Holland. He liked my work and asked me if I maybe had an idea for a short film we could make together before my return to Canada.

Photo: Lise Bechtold

Nico and I in the early days when we started working together.

Shortly before leaving Canada, I had the Montreal voice actor Peter Bierman record the English voice of David and, having some studio time left after the recording, I had asked him if he wouldn't mind doing a funny voice for a very short idea I had written years before when I was living in Spain. Peter, a very nice and talented young man, agreed and did a great job, speaking the few lines needed for my character in *The Killing of an Egg*, using a funny accent which people even still today remember and often act out when they meet me.

The Killing of an Egg was not only short (three minutes) but also very easy to make, again, with hardly any animation, and after Nico had heard the voice, he readily agreed to set up the production.

It's a "story inside a story": A person knocking on an egg, who, when a voice from inside the egg tells him to "stop that" loses control and smashes it to pieces. Then, when someone is heard knocking on the ceiling of his own dwelling, he says, "Stop that", in exactly the same voice, after which his space is smashed to pieces. The moment the protagonist answers the knocking from outside with the same voice you heard before, you know what's going to happen next. I could have stopped right there but decided to add another 30 seconds to finish the story.

It's a good example of a narration without a real punchline. Most of the animated cartoons from that time used linear storytelling to arrive at the punchline, an unexpected twist at the end.

Next to playing with space, I used the colour palette of an egg, yellow and white, to intensify the idea of being inside an egg.

I finished the animation just before my flight back to Montreal while Nico took care of the rest of the production. Nico and I continued our co-operation, making many films together over the years, but *The Killing of an Egg* became one of our biggest successes.

Still from The Killing of an Egg.

Before leaving Montreal in 1976, I had secured a project with the National Film Board to come back to after my Dutch spell. I had been asked by the Canadian Association of Mental Health to write a script for a short film about the influence of parents on their offspring and thus in February '77, I returned to my Film Board office to develop the backgrounds for the project.

However, in June of that year I was back in Europe again, this time at the festival of Annecy where *David* had won the Grand Prix ex equo with Co Hoedeman's *Sandcastle*.

With Co, Grand Prix ex equo, Annency, 1977.

In the summer of 1977, the municipal museum of The Hague had organized an exhibit of a group of residential graphic artists, including Heinz Edelmann, who, after the *Yellow Submarine*, had moved to The Hague; Gert Dunbar, responsible for the innovative House-style of the Dutch railways; Ootje Oxenaar, the designer of the very original, newly issued Dutch banknotes; and me, now also to be considered a resident of The Hague.

Partly based on the success of the exhibit, the city of The Hague offered to sponsor a new project. I proposed an idea for a film which was arranged as a triptych. It was called *On Land, at Sea, and in the Air,* another experiment with narrative space, in this case, telling three stories simultaneously.

In the film each one of the three characters stuck inside their individual panel touched upon similar themes, concepts like waking up, sudden rainfall, hunger, danger, mutual attraction. Only at the very end of the film were the characters of the panels connected, and the true identity of one of the three was revealed.

The making of *On Land, at Sea and In the Air* was an interesting process. I had met Karen Kommer, a young photographer at a student screen-

Storyboard page of
On Land, at Sea and in the Air.

ing event in The Hague, and together we moved into an attic apartment not far from the beach.

Each time part of the animation of *On Land, at Sea and In the Air* was finished, I would stuff the drawings in my packsack, jump on my bike and cycle through the dunes along the North Sea to the neighbouring seaside town of Katwijk where Meneer Van Beelen, an elderly bachelor, had constructed a 35mm animation camera-stand in his bedroom. Sitting next to him, explaining my intentions, Van Beelen would, frame by frame, shoot first one of the ten-minute-long segments from beginning to end (for instance the left panel where a grumpy character was asleep), having masked off the two other panels. Then on new rolls of film he would, in the same way, shoot each one of the bordering two segments. Needless to say, this was many years before computers arrived.

When the three segments of the film were shot and developed, I would take the rolls to the Bob Kommer Studios, owned by Karen's father, where his fellow engineers had built a flattop editing table which was capable of pulling two of my filmstrips at the same time through the sprocket holes. Thus, by shifting two of the three layers

Photo: Nico Crama

Meneer van Beelen at the camera stand in his bedroom.

around, we were able to do some rough editing. The film was, however, already very precisely planned; I had carefully timed the length of each connecting situation of the three individual stories and thus the final edit went quite smoothly.

Final image with rainfall, On Land, at Sea and in the Air.

Meanwhile, I had approached Willem Thijssen, a film producer in Amsterdam, with a plan for an animated feature. Willem was able to obtain a subsidy for developing my idea, and Karen and I moved to Ibiza, an island off the Spanish coast, for three weeks to quietly work on the script of Kikkerland/About Frogs.

To get acquainted with feature length projects, I brought along a couple of scripts of Hollywood classics *Double Indemnity, The Third Man and Casablanca,* solid screenplays that helped me with the construction of my film. For someone who never had to keep the audience's attention occupied for more than ten minutes, it was very useful to learn about the 'classics' practise of creating a proper build-up, of developing the various tension curves a feature needed, and, of course, the importance of working towards a surprise ending.

I work well in secluded places where I can concentrate on my self-imposed tasks. In Ibiza, I was devoted to working on my script, but we also relaxed, swam in the warm waters of the Mediterranean and tried out windsurfing, a popular sport on the island.

About Frogs was never produced. We couldn't secure a budget to finance the film. However, I haven't completely lost hope. Although I wrote the script more than 40 years ago, when I recently looked through it, I still felt that it had some potential. Some projects take a long time to mature but eventually get made, so we'll see.

In the spring of 1979, I got a phone call in the middle of the night from Hubert Tison, a Canadian producer at Société Radio-Canada, the French-Canadian branch of the CBC. Hubert had not realized that there was a six-hour time difference between Holland and Canada. I had a hard time trying to wake up and understand his proposal to come up with a short idea to be made at his studio in Montreal. Because of a tight deadline, Hubert explained that it should be an idea for a film that could be made fast—my specialty.

Amongst my notes, I found a simple idea for a short film called *Elbowing*, which Hubert liked. The story was a metaphor about using one's elbows to get to the top, after which one can't go any further, only down.

Elbowing shows a long line-up of men, all identically dressed and with the same features, passing on an elbow nudge. When the last one in the line-up receives the nudge, he loses his balance and falls down. Since you never see the feet of the group, you don't know what's below them; you only hear the cry of the falling person fading out to nothingness.

Subsequently, the whole group moves up one step to replace the missing person, and the nudging starts all over again. The act of passing on the nudges, however, is time and again interrupted by a colourful character

Still from Elbowing.

who holds up the process with his distracting behaviour. But in the end, he always steps back into the line-up and dutifully passes the nudge to the person standing next to him.

There wasn't much to animate in the film, just the one elbow-nudge, a couple of drawings which I would shift from one person to the next, plus the short, playful acts of the colourful character. Much of the action was told by the sound and the repetitive image of passing on the nudges, was helped along by the outstanding music score of my friend Normand Roger, the Montreal musician who, over the years, composed the music for many of my films.

Elbowing was one of those films where a lot of the action took place off-screen, saving precious animation time. I finished the film right on time.

While working at Radio Canada on *Elbowing,* I became friends with Frédéric Back, a lovely man and a great artist, who at the time was animating *Crac,* a film which two years later won an Oscar. (In 1988, Frédéric won his well-deserved second Oscar for his film *The Man Who Planted Trees.*)

Frédéric Back's cartoon about me always leaving for another country. At the time, I was working on an "upside-down" film.

Frédéric was also a very funny man, and during the times we worked side by side, he and I exchanged many cartoons.

When *Elbowing* was finished, I was approached by the National Film Board to come up with another idea for a "story-inside-a-story" film, leaning on the success of *Killing of an Egg.*

I wrote *The Same Old Story,* about a gentleman reading

a story about a lady who is threatened by a nasty character but is rescued by her hero. Then, the gentleman himself gets involved in a similar situation but is hesitant about being the hero. In the third and last episode, we see a real person (in pixelation) who closes the book in which the previous story was depicted. Then his doorbell suddenly rings, suggesting that behind his door he might be faced with the same challenge.

Stills from The Same Old Story.

I had this idea that at the premiere of the film, after this final pixelated character is disturbed by his doorbell, a loud bell would ring out in the theatre, making the audience look up...It's one of those nice ideas which, of course, has never been carried out.

☆ ☆ ☆

Back in Holland I was granted a subsidy for a project I had proposed called *Spotting a Cow*. I made it look like a "silhouette" film, although the black forms seen on screen were not real silhouettes, but rather black blotches painted on cels. In the film one hears the voice of a God-like narrator who, by throwing what looks like mud onto the screen, creates all kinds of black objects and characters which act out a personal drama.

The English Voice was narrated by Peter Bierman, the same talented actor of funny accents from my previous films *Killing of an Egg* and *David*. In the Dutch version, I hired a voice-actor who was known for doing a good imitation of the voice of Dries Van Agt, the Dutch prime minister at that time, who possessed an unctuous voice, and was often made fun of by many of my compatriots.

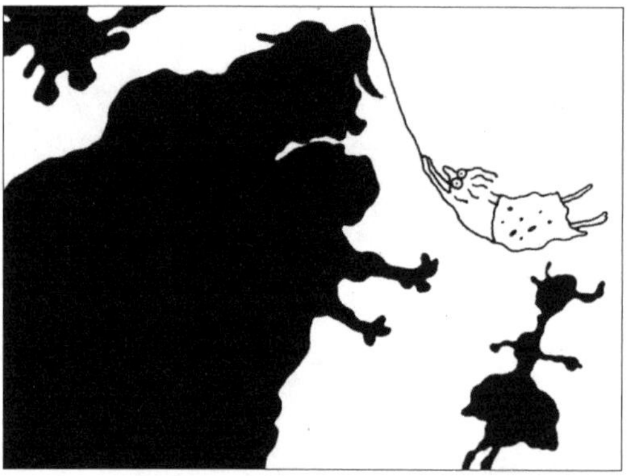

Still from Spotting a Cow.

The Foley sound was done at the Kommer studios by their very inventive sound engineers who, like me, enjoyed creating unusual sound effects. It was the first time that I brought in a pot with overcooked macaroni, which, when scooped up and dropped on a hard surface, made a great sound for mud being splashed onto the screen. The sounds we could extract from moist macaroni became the trademark for many of my later films.

During those years, alternating between more elaborate productions, I made two more three-minute films with my friend Nico Crama as producer. The first one, made in 1982 was called *Oh What a Knight*, a cartoon about a knight going to the rescue of a damsel in distress.

Discussing projects at the Ottawa animation festival with Nico.

Although it was written as a straightforward, funny cartoon, I inserted quite a few details, exploring the narrative space way of storytelling. For instance, each time the knight was hit, punched, or crashed to the ground, he fell apart in little pieces, bounced around like a bunch of metal cans, which then reassembled and restored him to his old form. Then off he went again to pursue his mission.

Storyboard page for Oh What a Knight.

At a certain point in the film, when the knight was carefully creeping around a mountain ridge, I cut very briefly to a modern cityscape in which I made him balance on the ledge of a very high building. Then I cut back to the mountain scene and let the persevering knight resume his action. It was an unexpected little interlude, but it proved to be quite effective.

Layout for mountain ledge scene of Oh What a Knight.

The second short I made with Nico was *Sunny Side Up,* which is very much a narrative space story. Like my old film *Air,* the screen was divided by a horizontal line. In this case, it represented the water surface in the middle of which a small island was situated, its image reflected on the other side of the line.

Opening credits of Sunny Side Up.

A castaway stuck on the island is seen trying to communicate with the outside world, the results of which, however, are only pictured at the top; no reflections are shown below the line. An unsuspecting viewer would, of course, assume that the island and its occupant were sitting on top of the waterline and that their reflections were mirrored at the bottom. At the end of the film, though, when the castaway jumps aboard a ship which comes to the rescue, the picture appears to be upside-down; the images on top proved to be only self-imagined illusions reflected in the water and by jumping aboard, he scatters the depiction of his final fantasy and drowns. A 180-degree turn of the image on screen then shows us that throughout the film, the castaway's reality was pictured at the bottom side, whereas his fantasies were reflected in the water at the top.

Igor Savin, whose music I loved for his 'Balkan sound', composed the film's haunting theme.

Short version of the storyboard for Sunny Side Up.

In 1985, I met Linda Wilson, and she invited me to join her in Vancouver to animate a couple of shorts for the 1986 Vancouver Expo. Under the circumstances, it was an offer hard to refuse. In Holland, I had become a little restless and going back to Canada, this time to Vancouver in beautiful British Columbia on the Pacific, seemed a very attractive option.

Linda had created a small studio not far from the renowned Emily Carr College, where we set up the production of the shorts which I had proposed for the upcoming event. The films were fun to do; they were simple and offbeat, and I shared the animation with two other animators whom we borrowed from International Rocketship, the studio of my good friend Marv Newland. At Rocketship, Marv and his colleagues survived by animating commercials and commissioned films, but in the festival circuit, they were known and loved for their wacky animated shorts.

It was during my time in Vancouver that I discovered Gary Larson, who became one of my favourite cartoonists. Even now, very many years later, I often take one of the Far Side albums from my bookcase and indulge in his humorous universe. He created some kind of crazy world I am slightly jealous of, for I felt I could step into it myself and join in with my own ideas, a challenging exercise for a cartoonist.

It was only when he looked outside that Warren suddenly remembered why he dropped his pants.

Hansel and Gretel in later years.

Two of my Larson-inspired cartoons.

Although I thought that it would be near impossible to go beyond the world of Larson's one-panel cartoons, in the nineties Marv succeeded in turning Gary Larson's *Tales of the Far Side* into two hilarious animated half-hours. Marv also understood the potential of Larson's whimsical framework in which he moved his characters. Although Larson's cartoons often depended on the captions which made his images so absurd, Marv succeeded in leaving out the words and getting the meaning of the gags across through the animation.

When tired of animating the Expo shorts, Linda, an excellent windsurfer, and I, a mere beginner, would take off and drive down to one of the lakes in the surrounding hills, where she would teach me the tricks of the trade. Fortunately, I was a good swimmer for I spent more time in the water than on top of the board.

Those were exciting but also very chaotic times and when the Expo shorts were done, I decided to return to Holland.

THE KASSEL YEARS

In the mid 80s, a group of students from Germany approached me at the Annecy Festival and invited me to teach in their Animation department at the University of Kassel. I have never been very interested in teaching and my initial reaction was to say no. But because the students were so nice and persistent, I agreed to go to Kassel for a week and give a workshop on storyboarding and storytelling.

Kassel is situated in the middle of Germany, in a rural landscape which was much favoured by the counts and dukes from past ages, who built their summer retreats between the surrounding hills. It was also close to the 'wall', running through the middle of Germany, separating the East from the West. Kassel itself is not a very beautiful town; much of the old centre was bombed during the war and the new housing developments are rather bland. The art department of the university, however, was built in Bauhaus style and sits in the beautiful Aue park, bordering the Orangerie, an old palace from the early 18th century, which was turned into a grand café and a museum of antiquities.

My first Kassel workshop turned out to be quite fun. I was easily won over to do some more teaching, filling in for their absent professor Jan Lenica, the famous Polish animator and poster designer, who had been promoted to the University of Berlin.

During my many visits to Kassel I discovered more and more interesting aspects of the town and its surroundings. About forty-five minutes drive north of our school there was one of the oldest forests of Europe, the 'Urwald'. It was quite an amazing feeling to walk amongst these old primeval trees and think back to their origin about 1000 years ago, when my forefathers and mothers roamed the very same woods.

A forty-five-minute drive west of Kassel brings one to the famous Eder dam where, in 1943, RAF Lancaster planes with specially designed 'bouncing bombs' destroyed the barrage in a spectacular operation which became known as 'The Dam Busters'. I had read the book and seen the film, but now I also visited the place with my students and crossed the legendary dam from one side to the other.

Kassel is also known for an exhibit of contemporary art called the Documenta, which takes place every five years. Each time, it is organized by a different leading curator from a different country. The exhibit is installed in the Fridericianum museum and in temporarily fabricated constructions, conveniently erected in the Aue park where the art department of our school was located.

Kassel is also the town where the Brothers Grimm lived and assembled their fairy tales. Dorothea Viehmann, the daughter of the owner of a tavern outside Kassel, where the Grimms often lingered, collected all kinds of tales from passing travellers and conveyed them to the eager ears of the two brothers. Since I often use plotlines of fairytales in my films, it was always a pleasure to visit the Grimm Museum in Kassel from where much of my inspiration originated.

My most exciting discovery in Kassel, however, was a gallery called Caricatura. It had regular exhibits of remarkably talented German cartoonists, often artists I had never heard of before.

The father of the comic strip as we know it was the German humorist and illustrator Wilhelm Busch (1832 - 1908). Inspired by Wilhelm Busch's stories of Max & Moritz, two naughty boys who played all kinds of pranks, the American cartoonist Rudolph Dirks developed *The Katzenjammer Kids,* multiple panel strips which initiated the 'funnies' in America.

Wilhelm Busch, Max & Moritz.

In some of the later generation of German cartoonists I recognized traces of Busch's neat style and humour. One of them is the fabulous draughtsmen F.K. Waechter, with his exquisite cross-hatching technique.

Other discoveries of German talent in the Caricatura Gallery were Ernst Kahl (also an accomplished musician), Michael Sowa, Bernd Pfarr and Rudi Hurzlmeier.

Many of my students were quite good aspiring filmmakers but they didn't have much of an art education. I remember that one student came up to me and was puzzled by my admiration for the art of Saul Steinberg. I had criticized the student's character design and he asked me why, when he drew a big nose on his character, I didn't think it was any good, whereas Steinberg's playful deformations were seen as great art.

F.K. Waechter.

I told him that first of all he should study Gerald Scarfe, a caricaturist famous for his 'nose' design, but that to recognize the artistic value of artists like Steinberg, you needed to know more about art in general.

I remembered that also for me, in my early days as a cartoonist, Steinberg was a bit of an enigma. I used to like funny cartoon characters like the ones in *The Katzenjammer Kids, Krazy Kat, Hagar the Horrible* and *The Wizard of Id* much more than the sophisticated drawings of Steinberg. It was only later that I not only began to appreciate the beauty of Steinberg's design but also the deeper meaning of his graphics, ideas which were very much based on my own interest, the use of narrative space.

Steinberg's vision of Manhattan and the rest of the world.

After almost two years of teaching workshops, during which one of my students won our first Oscar (in 1989 for 'Balance'), Kassel University decided to open up a full-time position for an animation professor. But when I was asked to apply, I declined because I felt that it would be in the way of my animation career. Also, I was comfortably living in Holland at the time, and I didn't want to move to Germany.

However, my students came up with a plan, proposing such a flexible teaching schedule that I agreed to join the other applicants bidding for the job. Although I was still a bit reluctant to take on the responsibility of a permanent job, the university, backed up by the support of my students and the boost of our Oscar success, chose me as the new Kassel animation professor.

It proved to have been a good decision to stay in Holland and not move my residency to Kassel because in January 1987, my rather unruly

Photo: Janek Czechowski

With the Kassel students.

seventeen-year-old daughter Anouk wanted to leave home (her mother's house) and asked if she could maybe move in with me. I said yes, of course, but because I hadn't lived with my children since they were three and four years old, it meant quite a change in my life.

On top of that, Anouk had just split up with her boyfriend and was in quite an emotional state of mind. Fortunately, soon after she moved in with me, she met this handsome young student who often walked his dog on the street below her window, and she quickly recovered from her misery. Stef and Anouk stayed together for many years, and he became the father of her two children.

Later that year I was invited as a jury member for the Hiroshima Animation Festival. It was a very special occasion because I was asked to be on the jury with Osamu Tezuka, the 'father' of manga. Tezuka was a lovely and very erudite man, who, along with the famous Japanese puppet animator Kihachirō Kawamoto, had invited to show me, my Vancouver friend Linda and the Russian animator Yuri Norstein around Japan's old capital, Kyoto. It was a wonderful visit. Both Tezuka and Kawamoto were great ambassadors of their culture, and we were welcomed in the beautiful gardens and hidden monasteries our hosts had access to, and enjoyed delicious meals in the old city, conversing in sign language with the geishas which were dispersed amongst us at the table.

Kyoto visit with Osamu Tezuka (with beret), Yuri Norstein (bending over) and Kirachiro Kawamoto (holding bag).

In November 1987, I went to Hollywood for the first time. Amidst the other recipients, many of whom were old Disney veterans, I was given the Annie Award for my 'distinguished contribution to the art of animation'. My friend Marv Newland presented the award to me with a funny speech which, I remember, seemed to puzzle most of the elderly crowd who were unfamiliar with Marv's quirky sense of humour.

It was the first of six Lifetime Achievement Awards I received over the years, although most of the other ones were given when I was much older, at a time in my life when, I imagine, I was either supposed to stop making films or wasn't expected to live much longer.

And indeed, in January '89, I had an accident which almost cost my life.

Riding back home on my bicycle from a late-night party with friends in The Hague, a drunken driver, asleep at the wheel, drove his big Volvo straight into me. I broke all my ribs on the left side of my body and my left shoulder blade. Also, one of the ribs pierced my lung, which collapsed. An ambulance was called, and I was brought to a nearby hospital while the police woke the driver and took him away.

I have fallen a lot during my life (still do, actually), usually from my bike, though except for a broken toe and a sprained wrist, I was never badly hurt. But this accident felt serious, and I clearly needed some help to get my body back in shape. I was surprised to learn, however, that other than giving me some painkillers, the doctors were not going to do any surgery; I had to do the healing all by myself. And although it was a painful process (the painkillers didn't much help) my rib withdrew from my lung which then neatly closed up and all the other ribs and the broken shoulder blade slowly moved back into place. After about four weeks, I was back at my animation desk

Still from Death and the Writer.

and could continue the film I had been working on, appropriately called *Death and the Writer*.

While that was the most serious accident, it's not the only one worth noting.

Once in Montreal, going down a hill on my way to the Film Board, a large truck passing me on the left suddenly, without signalling, pulled to the right into a parking lot, cutting me off completely by surprise. I still remember swerving, trying to avoid the truck's big rear wheels, then being hurled over my handlebars onto the rough pavement, landing on my face. I had a bloody face, and nothing was broken, but to my horror, when I opened my eyes, I only saw white, I was completely blind. Fortunately, this condition lasted only about thirty seconds; then slowly, my sight came back.

Not so long after, I was diagnosed with glaucoma, an eye disease that has to do with tension in the optical nerve. There are many reasons people get glaucoma, but one is that it might occur after a shock. And being briefly blinded was clearly caused by shock. My glaucoma is now stabilized, and although my left eye has only peripheral vision, I can see well enough to enjoy the beauty of our surroundings, drive a car, read a book, and animate films.

The second bicycle accident I remember well was of a more recent date, and although maybe painful, not of a dangerous nature; in retrospect, it was really kind of an odd incident.

One late afternoon, riding back on my old bike from a swim in the river not far from where I now live in France, carrying a heavy backpack with towels, a beach chair and a parasol on my back, the slope of a small road appeared just too steep for my strength. Coming to a full stop, I lost my balance and slowly fell over, landing headfirst in a two-meter-deep ditch full of brambles.

There I was, with no headgear, wearing only a t-shirt and short pants, stuck upside down in the brambles full of thorns with the bike and heavy backpack pressing down on me; I had also lost my glasses.

It took me more than half an hour to very slowly free my arms from the thorns, grab my glasses, push the bike and backpack up and off my body, and then climb out of the ditch. Covered in bloody scratches, I walked my bike up the hill back home. I hope my next fall will be an ordinary one, maybe a little blood, a flat tire and bent handlebars, but nothing to write home about.

* * *

On occasion, following what felt like 'near death' situations (such as once, deep in thought, I crossed an unprotected level crossing, right after which a train rushed by), I did sometimes wonder if the awareness of being alive might just be a fantasy, that the image of me still amongst the living might soon fade away, reality would kick in and I'd be gone.

Rough storyboard page of The Boy who saw the Iceberg, *displaying the two sides of the narrative.*

Partly based on this idea, I made the film *The Boy Who Saw the Iceberg*. It tells the story of a little boy with a strong imagination who, whenever a situation occurs that he doesn't want to face; lets his fantasy take over. In the film, the screen is divided in two: when the film begins, the animated images on the right side are exact copies of the ones on the left, both showing the real world in which the boy lives.

But when he feels threatened, the left side of the screen continues to show the actual facts of his life, while the right side displays the boy's imagination, his escape from the harsh reality he wants to avoid. His fantasies, however, never last, and after a short spell of an adventurous nature, are cut off by noisy reminders of the present—alarm clocks, honking horns, school bells. They all roughly wake the boy from his reveries and bring him back to reality. Both sides of the screen show the same image again.

The split-screen of The Boy Who Saw the Iceberg.
On the left is reality, and on the right the boy's fantasy.
The Boy Who Saw the Iceberg (2000) | Version 213365 / Dir. Paul Driessen

In the second part of the film, the boy and his family find themselves aboard a big ship that looks very much like the Titanic. When it goes down, as we all know the Titanic did, the little boy desperately unleashes his fantasies, trying to extend his life through the sheer force of his imagination. He makes it last for a little while longer, but eventually he acknowledges his defeat, climbs back into bed and pulls his blankets over his head, as little boys do when they want to hide. The right side of the screen turns back to reality, and the end credits slowly creep up over the now two identical panels, both showing the vast empty ocean where the big ship went down.

Storyboard page from The Boy Who Saw the Iceberg.

In addition to my implementation of narrative space in the film—the two different points of view in the story— and the use of the Titanic as a reference, I also hinted at the idea that we might be dead but, for a little while, we don't know it yet.

During their heyday in the 30s, the surrealists invented a playful little game they called *cadavre exquis* in which each member of a collective of artists were given the end of a phrase or part of a design from which the next person in the group was intended to continue the writing or drawing, without knowing what the previous artists had done before.

Based on that idea, Marv Newland produced the ten-minute film *Anijam*, a project in which each of twenty-two animators selected from all over the world, myself included, were given either the first or the last drawing of a fifteen-second animated segment done by another animator, which would then become the last or first drawing of their own fifteen-second piece. None of us knew what the animation before or after was like.

Poster for Anijam.

The film was quite successful. All the animators involved had enjoyed making up little stories known only to themselves, as well as the gratification of the outcome.

Marv, who had become a dear friend, and I discussed ideas for a project in the same vein as *Anijam* on one of our travels from the Annecy Festival to Holland. Marv came up with a plan in which all members of a small select group of animators would be given an identical thirty-second soundtrack, and each one would animate a segment according to their personal interpretation of the soundtrack. The soundtrack, however, would be of a rather adult quality, a suggestive progression of crazy sounds leading up to some kind of orgiastic finale.

Photo: Karen Kommer

Sound session with Marv Newland for Pink Komkommer.

We approached the Bob Kommer Studios in The Hague, where I had made quite a few of my previous soundtracks, and since we didn't have a budget, we explained the idea to them with the promise that if the film made some money, they would be reimbursed from the revenues. The studio agreed, and thus Marv and I tried our hand at creating a succession of pornographic sounding effects which would in the end be the guideline for a selection of animators who we thought might be good candidates for this enterprise.

We created all kinds of sound effects which encapsulated the nature of the project: squeaking bedsprings, dripping and gushing watery sounds, and of course, my trademark sound effects produced from sopping, overcooked macaroni.

We brought in our Scottish friend Colin Nawrot, a.k.a. The Amazing Mister Wonderful, who not only often acted as cameraman and assisted with tracing and painting the animation cels of most of my Dutch independent shorts, but was also indispensable at the sound sessions of my films. Teaming up with Karen, the two of them created very convincing panting and moaning sounds, which, I remember, made me slightly uncomfortable, since we'd been very close friends for many years.

Marv then approached seven renowned animators for the project, all artists who worked in different styles. He appointed one of them, the Canadian Chris Hinton, to connect each of the segments with a creation of his own. Chris was also asked to bring his characters into play for the final scene, applying once more the suggestive soundtrack. Quite a few of our selected animators contributed non-pornographic visuals to the sound, which made the film even funnier than we had anticipated.

Because of the generous gesture of the Bob Kommer Studios to accommodate us with their sound studio, Marv called the film *Pink Komkommer* (*komkommer* meaning 'cucumber' in Dutch).

My Pink Komkommer *segment.*

Sara Petty's Pink Komkommer *segment.*

Chris Hinton's Pink Komkommer *segment.*

Marv's Pink Komkommer *segment.*

In 1989, at the animation festival in Varna, Bulgaria, I met the Czech illustrator-animator Michaela Pavlatova. The Czechs have a great graphic arts tradition, often working in a particular style I've been very fond of since first visiting the Prague studios in 1969. Michaela was not only a wonderful draughtswoman but also a very funny person. We became good friends, and in 1989 I invited Michaela to The Hague to write and animate an *Uncles & Aunts* episode, as part of a series of short cartoons Nico Crama and I had in production.

The basic idea of *Uncles & Aunts* was portraying a succession of 'drawn' family photographs, pictures of family settings such as one finds in traditional photo albums. Those photographs were generally accompanied by a caption, often a humorous interpretation of the photographic image.

My storyboard for an episode of Uncles & Aunts.

In *Uncles & Aunts* all the snapshots were intended to be very limited animated cartoons, assisted by silly captions, kind of tongue-in-cheek descriptions of the imagery. I had already made two *Uncles & Aunts* myself and, as a story exercise, had also given my Kassel students the assignment to write one of their own. Although it seemed easy to come up with funny little family stories, it proved quite difficult to make them sufficiently snappy to keep up with the spirit of the series.

Michaela, however, being an exceptional artist with a wacky sense of humour, made a great *Uncles & Aunts*, even funnier than all the other ones made so far.

Still from one of my Uncles & Aunts *episodes.*

Michaela Pavlatova's Uncles & Aunts.

In November 1989, just after the wall had fallen, I visited Michaela in her Prague studio. One evening she took me to a concert in the beautiful old theatre in the centre of town where the musician she often worked with and his friends were giving a concert. At a certain point, the singer, accompanied by his guitar, sang a kind of 'freedom' ballad and when the song was finished, he stood up and pointed to the theatre's front balcony. There, in the spotlight, stood Vaclav Havel, who was going to be Czechoslovakia's new president, waving at the exuberant crowd.

Toasting Havel that day in Prague felt like a truly historical event, like when my father as a child saw the Kaiser of Germany, the King of England and the Tsar of Russia riding by, and I, as an eight-year-old, saw Stalin saluting the tanks of the red army rolling by.

The following year, in the summer of 1990, the Japanese television company NHK contacted Nico Crama and me with a proposal for an animated project. The assignment was for a half-hour animated movie to be used as the opening film at the cinema in Holland-Nagasaki Village, a newly erected theme park on an island outside the city of Nagasaki. This theme park was being built to celebrate the almost 400 years of trade between Japan and The Netherlands, and inside one of the many replicas of old Dutch canal houses, there was a cinema for shows about Holland.

The project we presented to NHK, *The Water People,* was a very Dutch idea about a small kingdom situated in a pond, surrounded by a dike, not to keep the water out but to keep it in. This territory was inhabited by people who lived partly above and partly below the water's surface. As the main storyline, I used the legend of Hans Brinker, the boy who kept the water out (in this case, 'in') by putting his finger in the dike.

The narrative space approach I applied to this film was the division of the action which was either seen above or below the water surface; but one never saw the action in both halves at the same time. This gave me the opportunity to create many playful situations.

Still from The Water People *showing the action above the waterline.*

Still from The Water People *showing the action below the waterline.*

For instance, in one of the early scenes of the film, Mother Brinker inserts a slice of bread in the underwater toaster and pours tea into a cup below the water's surface. The toast pops up through the surface to be caught and eaten by Father Brinker. Subsequently, Father Brinker lifts his filled cup from below the water surface and drinks his tea. When cut to the part below the waterline, which was covered up in the previous shot, we see the couple's son, Hans Brinker, sitting at the breakfast table, too small to appear above the water surface. This situation, of course, allowed me to play out some pranks with the mischievous little boy.

Before landing my Kassel job I had never made much money with my short personal films and could never really afford to pay for the flights back and forth from Canada to Holland, to work on projects which demanded my presence on either side of the ocean. I had figured out a system, though, involving the festivals which very often invited me to represent my films. There was some general arrangement that if your film was in competition, either the festivals or the institutions who had produced the film, would offer to fly you over. As my films were very often accepted in the competitive category, I just had to make sure that I had the next project waiting for me in the country not too far from the festival where one of my films was being shown.

Looking back, it's interesting to see that this system and the lure of these free trips for many, many years not only allowed me to continue making personal films but also pushed my creative output, challenging me to come up with new ideas of interest to sponsors. They would, in turn, send my films to festivals who would invite me. But when I became an animation professor in Kassel, for the first time in my life I had a regular salary. This, of course, made me much more independent in my movements, as I could now easily pay for my own trips.

I recently checked the level of my productivity 'before,' 'during,' and 'after' Kassel and it seems that the teaching job didn't really slow down my work as a filmmaker. I still made about one animated short every two years.

Curiously, only after my retirement from Kassel in 2005 did my output decrease. I believe that this was due to two reasons: First, my projects became more complex, and the films needed to be longer to be understood. Also, I began more and more to enjoy my art, the boundless possibilities of drawn animation. Before, I had always tried to find shortcuts, ways to avoid making too many drawings. Once retired, I was able to indulge in the execution of my animated characters. I put a lot of my time and energy into experimenting with the premise of how much one can stretch, bounce, and twist one's characters, reduce them to a line, a bunch of hair, or merely a pair of eyes, or make them disappear and pop up again. In animation, almost anything goes, as long as there's some follow-up in the related images to help the audience keep up with the flow of things.

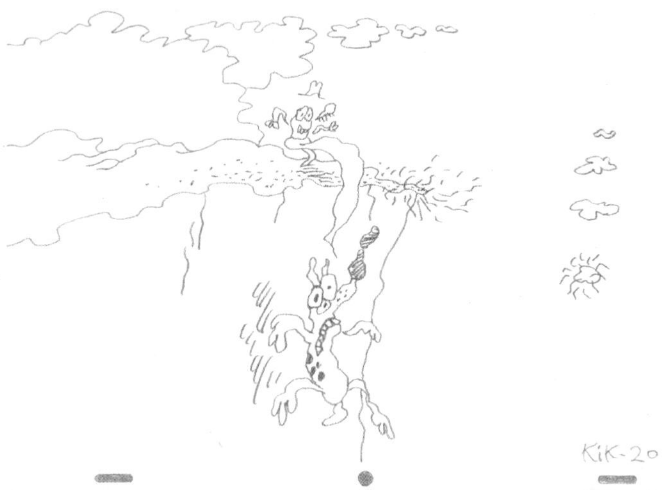

Drawing from Oedipus *showing a "stretched" character.*

Secondly, during the eighties and nineties, throughout the West, economy-driven governments started to cut back in 'culture'. Since short films by and large have no commercial value, they rely heavily on subsidies. It became increasingly difficult for producers of independent shorts to find the money for artistic personal films like mine.

In August 1990, I met Diane, my future wife, at the Ottawa Animation Festival. It was hard to resist her enchanting smile, and because our interest in each other was mutual, we made plans for me to move back to Canada. Diane, who came from a large French-Canadian family in northern Ontario, was running a small advertising agency in Ottawa with two partners. She grew up in an area where a dynamic artistic community played a significant role in the struggle to keep the French-Canadian culture alive in the predominantly English-speaking province of Ontario. Although Diane was fluently bilingual when I met her, she told me that she had hardly spoken any English until she picked it up in her early twenties.

Photo: David O'Malley

Diane and her enchanting smile.

My plan to move back to Canada had some consequences, of course. I had to organize work in Canada and figure out how to keep my job as a full-time professor in Kassel. Both Canada and Kassel helped me out. At the same festival where I met Diane, I had talked to Marcy Page, a newly appointed producer at the English Animation department of the National Film Board of Canada, who was looking for ideas for films which could be finalized on the Board's, still primitive, computer system. We agreed on *The End of the World in 4 Seasons*, a multi-screen project in which each season of the year was portrayed by a total of eight little stories together on screen, representative of that particular season.

The plan was that I would animate each one of the eight panels individually in the centre of my drawing board, after which the Film Board's computer would position all the panels in their proper places.

Meanwhile, my Kassel students had won a second Oscar (Thomas Stellmach and Ty Montgomery with their short film Quest), and because of this success, adjusting my teaching schedule to less frequent visits to the

Positioning of the 'spring' panels of The End of the World in 4 Seasons.

Positioning of the 'winter' panels of The End of the World in 4 Seasons.

'Winter' still from The End of the World in 4 Seasons.

school was quietly agreed on. Instead of spending my usual one week a month in Kassel I would visit the school for two weeks every two months, a timespan that would still come up to the mandatory teaching of eight hours a week.

But before moving back to Canada, I still had to finish *The Water People,* the project for the Japanese television station NHK. Mark Reijnders, a Dutch animation friend and computer wizard, helped us find a good computer test program for the film. Till the end of the eighties, most animators still shot their line-tests on 16mm cameras or used malfunctioning video machines. It was still early in the development of computer programs for animation, and Mark ended up finding us an Amiga line-test program which suited our needs.

The Bob Kommer Studios had provided me with space on the top floor of their building, and thus, we had room to hire a few people to work on the premises. Two professionals, Piet Kroon and Jan Sanctorum, assisted by a young Kris van Alphen, joined us to make up the animation team. The illustrator Georgien Overwater, with whom I had worked on some of my other projects, created the beautiful backgrounds for the film, mixing a lot of moisture into her colours for the 'wet look' and fabricating the 'frozen over' surfaces by scratching ice patterns onto thinly painted cels.

Halfway through the production, NHK asked if we could also make a shorter version of the film. It was an interesting challenge for me to basically tell the same story in only half the time. Although some of the fun scenes had to be left out, in the end, the short version was certainly as enjoyable as the long one. We had to extend the production time somewhat, but finally, in the summer of 1992, *The Water People* was finished, and Diane and I moved to Montreal, the city we both knew quite well and loved.

Crew of The Water People.

FULL CIRCLE

Diane and I found an apartment in Outremont, a district typical of Montreal with a mixture of English and French Canadians, a large Greek population and an extensive orthodox Jewish community. Close by were many Greek restaurants, offering scrumptious Greek food, and a few streets away from our place was a famous bagelry, which was open 24 hours a day. There was also some competition from a New York bagelry in the neighbourhood which sold the NY style bagels, but everyone agreed that the Montreal bagels on Rue St. Viateur were hard to beat. When staying abroad, it's the Montreal bagel which I miss the most.

While my daughter Anouk studied to be an actress in Holland and after graduation joined the successful experimental theatre troupe 'Het Barre Land', my son Kaj, who was born in Canada, came over for a year to continue his film studies at Dawson College in Montreal.

Anouk at graduation of her theatre school.

Although it must have been quite difficult for him to be plunged into North American life far from home, Kaj did very well and even won the Most Promising Student of his Year award. I do, nonetheless, still regret that I probably didn't pay enough attention to him as a responsible father should have, preoccupied as I was adjusting to my own new life with Diane. But I think that Kaj, being a generous young man, forgave me for my neglect. After returning to Holland, Kaj started a successful career as a live-action film director, working on children's series for television and occasionally making independent shorts.

☆ ☆ ☆

1996 was a busy and eventful year for us. Diane and I bought a house in the centre of Montreal, then moved to the south of France for the summer and, later that year, we decided to get married. Since the Montreal city hall didn't seem a very appealing place for such a romantic event, we embarked on a four-hour drive south to the picturesque US town of Montpelier, Vermont, for the occasion. Upon arrival we were directed to the municipality's old library where an authorized official, a tall, bearded man called Barny Bloom pronounced us husband and wife.

The only drawback of our decision to get married in the town of that name was that when we later installed ourselves in our little village in southern France, there was considerable confusion when we had to get our papers in order. All our official documents went through the nearby city of Montpellier, from which the New Englanders had borrowed the name Montpelier, honouring the country of France for defeating the British during the war of the American Independence. Explaining this particular event in the history of America to the French authorities was not an easy task, but when we mentioned that North America had not only appropriated Montpelier from the old country but also Paris, a town in the state of Texas, the local authorities were humoured and signed the necessary papers required for our residency. French being Diane's mother tongue and the French-Canadian accent being charming to the French was, of course, very helpful when tackling the notoriously rigid French bureaucracy.

Because neither of us had good memories of dates, we decided to choose a wedding day easy to remember. Our first choice was the sixth of December, St Nicolas night in Holland, when the good Saint rides over the rooftops on his dappled horse and helped by his black servants (now banned as politically incorrect), drops presents through the chimneys into the shoes of well-behaved children. In return, the children put carrots in their shoes the night before as snacks for the horse.

However, on the sixth of December, 1989, a horrible incident took place at École Polytechnique, an engineering school affiliated with the Université de Montreal—a crazed young misogynist burst into a classroom waving a gun and, taking all the female students aside, killed fourteen young women and then took his own life.

Diane and I decided to pick the day before, December the fifth, also a memorable but more innocent date, the day St Nicolas, sailing from Spain, arrives at the Dutch shores. (At times, I'm still confused about which date it is, though.)

Two years later, in January 1998, a devastating ice storm swept through the province of Québec and particularly ravaged the island of Montreal, the place where we lived. Strong winds accompanied by freezing rain cut off Montreal's electricity. The weight of the ice accumulating on the electric wires broke down almost all of the pylons carrying electricity to the island. Since most of the Canadian heating systems relied on electrical power, temperatures in houses started to drop at a scary rate. Some houses had fireplaces, which helped out for a little while, but lots of homes had to be evacuated and all over Montreal generator-heated centres were set up where people could find refuge. In addition to the calamity, the bridges leading onto the island of Montreal, the arteries of food supply, closed down one after the other because, covered in ice, they became too dangerous to cross.

On the first day of the ice storm, when night fell and temperatures started to plummet, we lit up the many candles Diane had accumulated for emergencies and for a while managed to keep our living room at a reasonable temperature. We invited some friends who were stuck at homes without any heat, and after warming up a large pot of soup on our gas stove, we spent the evening eating, drinking, and playing board games till far into the night. Then we went to bed fully clothed and covered with layers of blankets to wait out our ordeal while the temperatures outside kept dropping.

We were lucky that the area where we lived was deprived of electricity for only forty-eight hours. In lots of places in the city there was no heat supply for days on end, sometimes weeks.

I remember that when it was all over, we visited the Mount-Royal Park in the centre of town. We were appalled by the terrible toll the storm had taken on the trees, many of which had collapsed, weighted down by the burden of the ice clinging to their branches.

In the fall of the same year, Queen Beatrix of the Netherlands had prepared a state visit to Russia to meet with President Yeltsin. As is the custom on these occasions, the queen brings with her an entourage of musicians, clowns and artists to make the event more festive. For some reason I also appeared on the list of entertainers, and I didn't hesitate to grab the chance to visit the country I hadn't been back to since my childhood.

Upon arrival in Moscow, our group was invited to the Dutch embassy which was still at the same location as when it was founded in the early 40s. The staff was quite impressed by my claim to have lived in the same building fifty years earlier, but when I expressed my wish to visit the ambassador's quarters (where, at the time we had had our dancing and singing lessons with Ivan Ivanovich and Nicolai Nicolaevich) the request made them rather uncomfortable. Asking for access to the privacy of the ageing conservative ambassador, unknown to me, was obviously considered intrusive, a bit too much to ask.

Later that day, our delegation was invited to the opening of a photo exhibit where, amongst other prominent people, I was introduced to the wife of the Dutch ambassador, Clara van Pallandt. She happened to be the daughter of the ambassador from the last year of my father's tenure in Moscow. So, we talked about the old days and in the end, she invited me to have coffee in her living quarters. The large room with the shiny parquet floors where we had performed our Russian dances still looked the same as I remembered from my childhood, and the grand piano on which our teacher Nicolaevich had taught us Russian songs was still there.

Clara also talked about her older brother Frederik who, together with his Danish wife Nina, had formed the folk duo Nina & Frederik, popular in the 50s and the early 60s. I remember that an old friend of our parents from the war, a woman we called *Tante Waf* (Dutch for "woof") because of her two enormous white Samoyed dogs, who often came to visit us in Rotterdam, loved the sweet calypso songs of the duo. I guess we all did at that time until the Beatles burst in with a different kind of sound.

In the week that followed, the embassy lent me a car with driver and on one of my trips I visited Tamillino, a small village about thirty kilometers from Moscow where, in a typical Russian dacha, we had spent many a summer. With the help of a translator, I asked an old villager if he maybe knew the red-haired Ludmilla, a young woman I remembered who my parents had hired at the time for cooking and cleaning. Oh yes, he said, everybody in the village knew Ludmilla, but unfortunately, she had died the week before.

On the way back from Tamillino I dropped in at the studio of my old animation friend Yuri Norstein, where Yuri and his staff welcomed me with a hearty Russian meal, nicely diluted with wine and vodka. When our stomachs were full, Yuri dressed me up in the coat he used as a prop for his film *The Overcoat* based on the story by Gogol. Yuri was involved in an ongoing struggle with the authorities to get the project financed. Although large segments of *The Overcoat* were shown at various festivals (all very impressive), I don't think that Yuri has ever managed to finish the film.

Photo: Ton Crone

With Yuri Norstein, dressed in the coat used as prop in his film The Overcoat.

It was great having had the opportunity to return to the places of my childhood in such a luxurious fashion. Queen Beatrix, however, never showed up. Apparently, Yeltsin fell sick, and her visit was cancelled.

In the year 2000, my film *3 Misses* was nominated for an Oscar. Although my Kassel students had already been nominated twice (and had won the Oscar both times) it was a first for me. Four of our friends were also nominated that year: the Canadians Wendy Tilby and Amanda Forbis for *When the Day Breaks* and Torill Kove for *My Grandmother Ironed the King's Shirts,* both Film Board productions, and our Russian friend Alexandre Petrov, one of the great masters of animation-painted-on-glass, with his film *The Old Man and the Sea.*

The National Film Board of Canada had hired the traditional limousine to get their nominees to the Oscar venue, but my film was produced by

CinéTé Productions in the Netherlands and being late in the game, all the limousines were gone when we applied for this status vehicle. We ended up travelling in a Volkswagen van, which followed the same route as the long line of limousines until, about a block away from the theatre's entrance, we were diverted to the parking lot in the back. While the limousines stopped at the red carpet, where the passengers who stepped out were besieged by masses of celebrity-seeking photographers, nobody took much notice of people like us who walked in from the parking lot behind the theatre. But in the end, during the long drive through a large section of the poorer parts of Hollywood, where crowds of residents stared at the spectacle, sitting in an unobtrusive van felt a little more comfortable than being shown off inside the golden cage of a luxury limousine.

When the envelope was opened and it was announced that Alexandre had won the Oscar for his *Old Man and the Sea* I was very relieved that it wasn't me who had to get onto the stage in front of millions of spectators and mumble something coherent, trying to remember whom to thank. I've been on stage on many occasions for smaller celebrations and was never very good at thanking all the right people.

Diane and I at the Oscars, 2000.

What I liked best about the hoopla of an Oscar nomination was that shortly after the event, I was invited to become a member of the Academy. The yearly fee was quite high but every year I would get a whole bunch of DVDs, not only from my own category, Short & Feature Animation, but also from production companies of all the other categories. At the end of the race, when the nominations are announced, members of all categories have the opportunity to vote for any of the nominated films.

3 Misses, the film I was nominated for, had an interesting history. The story is about three ladies in distress: the first lady is losing her balance at the edge of a building and plunges down to the busy street below; the second lady is tied-up on a train track while a train is approaching; and the third lady is Snow White, in danger of being poisoned by the witch. For each one of the three ladies, a clumsy male hero is running to their rescue, in the end all failing in their attempts to save the poor women (since it's a cartoon, the mishaps are more funny than sad).

In my original script, one of the three stories I had written was about two explorers in the jungle, one of whom was captured by natives and was being boiled in a pot (eventually, his clumsy friend comes to the rescue, but

Stills from 3 Misses.

he also ultimately fails). Clare Kitson of Britain's famed Channel-4 who had offered to coproduce the film wrote to me that, because of her country's colonial history, boiling someone in a pot surrounded by natives would cause an outcry in the UK and that, unless I replaced the pot boiling by another story, regretfully she would have to withdraw her participation in the production.

Although I really liked my ending of the man in the pot (in the last scene, the friend who failed to save his colleague is sharing his meal with the natives sitting around the pot and lifting a bone from the soup says: "Dr. Livingstone I presume?") I replaced the story by introducing a clumsy prince who tries to rescue Snow White. Again, like his two predecessors, the prince fails, in this case, because he mixes up Snow White with Cinderella.

I must admit that I was at first a little hurt by the fact that my artistic integrity was interfered with, but in the end, I don't think that the initial version of consuming old Dr. Livingstone would have led to an Oscar nomination.

Many years later, when I made *The Origin of Sound,* a film packed with short cartoons in bad taste, I included an even worse pot-boiling scene in one of the rather distasteful stories (something to do with natives and the size of private parts). But although the audience might vaguely sense what's going on, I made sure that the cartoon was somewhere in the background during the end credits and not very clearly seen.

Storyboard page for the politically incorrect "pot-boiling" scene.

Not long after my Oscar nomination, I met the legendary stop-motion pioneer Ray Harryhausen, who introduced me to his wife Diana Livingstone Bruce. Her great great (great?) grandfather, she said, was the real Dr. Livingstone. I didn't venture to tell her about my version of her ancestor's fate.

In 2001, the Dutch film producer Gerrit Visser, whom I knew from way back when he worked at the same studio where I started my animation career, proposed to make a documentary about my life and films, called *Paul Driessen Inside-out*. It was to be shot both in Montreal, my main residence, and in the south of France, where we spent the summer months.

The first part of the shoot was planned for Montreal in winter, where, in the opening stage of the film, I was supposed to trudge through the snow. It was going to be a scene from where we would cut to the winter season of my film *The End of the World in 4 Seasons*, a sequence full of images of snow and ice. However, when the film crew arrived in Montreal in January 2002, it was one of those rare Canadian winters with very little snow. We managed to scrape some of the powdery stuff together, though, and in the end the scene looked quite convincing.

We were more fortunate with the summer shoot, where we used some images from the summer season of the same film connecting me to a very summery beach on the Mediterranean, about an hour's drive from our house in France. Diane, a painter and graphic artist, made the lovely backgrounds for the film's title sequence.

Being asked to be the subject of a documentary was, of course flattering, but I'm not sure if Diane and I, appearing in little sketches created to fit in with the animation of some of my films, was a good idea; we might be good artists and animators, but we were clearly not great actors.

☆ ☆ ☆

In the summer of 1997, my mother died, and a few years later, in March 2001, my father followed. They were lovely parents and I have very good memories of them when growing up but unfortunately in later years they grew apart and, in the end, they were quite unhappy in each other's company. The sad thing is that I really have to try hard to remember them as the caring, enterprising and lovable people they were instead of the strong and lingering image of their unhappiness.

Olga (my parent's Russian teacher), my mother and my father lost in the fog of their later years.

About a year after my father's death new life arrived in the Driessen family. When unexpectedly the doorbell rang at our Montreal home in March 2002, to my surprise my daughter Anouk stood on the doorstep, my first grandchild in her arms—Lola Bo Chinouk Gietertje (the latter meaning 'little watering can,' just a fun kind of name). Without my knowledge, Anouk and Diane had organized a surprise visit, secretly planning her trip from Amsterdam to Montreal, shortly after Lola was born.

Not long after, my son Kaj and his girlfriend Joyce produced Milan, and about a year later two more siblings arrived, Bing, fathered by 'big' Kaj, and 'little' Kaj, mothered by Anouk. They were all close to each other, and in their first few years, the whole bunch often came to France to spend the summer in our large house in the south.

Gummbah's cartoon, referring to the choice of unusual names.

Photo: Diane Dauphinais

Anouk visiting in France holding Lola Gietertje and Milan.

Photo: Diane Dauphinais

Kaj's blond kids Bing and Milan with Anouk's dark haired kids Lola and 'little' Kaj in the bathtub in our home in France.

In 2005, Kaj and I, both professional filmmakers at the time, made plans to make a film together, half animated, half live-action.

I wrote the script called *The 7 Brothers,* a story which featured not only the two Grimm brothers we know of, but seven brothers of that name. These 7 brothers walked through the cobbled streets of an old town, looking for clues which might inspire them to come up with fairy tales. The fairy tales, shown as animated sketches on screen, looked like the ones we're familiar with, but every one of them ended quite differently from the original versions of the tales. The seven brothers themselves were shot in live action, directed by Kaj; I animated the seven fairytales each of the brothers came up with.

Kaj and I, during the shoot of The 7 Brothers.

The 7 Brothers: *Rapunzel.*

Animated image from The 7 Brothers.

My Dutch-Belgian friend Willem Thijssen, who had produced *3 Misses,* was interested in the project, and found excellent decor for the live-action shoot in Lier, a small village in Belgium. As an animator, working at a slow craft, I was amazed how quickly Kaj and his crew changed the old Flemish convent of Lier into a medieval town with a working bell tower and

Photo: Xavier Rombouts

Still from The 7 Brothers – *the brothers writing down their stories.*

full of props we needed as inspirational objects for the brothers. Our seven brothers were seven elderly Belgian actors. The filming of their assigned roles was completed in only two days. Then the cameras stopped rolling, the film was put in cans, everything was taken down and the town looked as if none of the extended Grimm family had ever set foot in it.

The 7 Brothers premiered at the film festival in Poznan, a nice old town in the mid/east of Poland. Kaj travelled to Poznan to represent the film and there he met Marta, a lovely young woman who was part of the organization of the festival. They fell in love, married, and in 2015 Marta gave birth to my fifth grandchild, Mieszko Poznan, named after the city of their romantic encounter.

Early in the 2000s, I finally found a publisher, Les 400 Coups, interested in my Fiddle Fumble Stories, which I had written back in 1969 when living in Vinaroz. The first two collections were published in black and white, and a few years later, two more in monochrome colours.

The Fiddle Fumble stories are playful, narrative space ideas in which, through little puzzles and visual concepts, young readers are confronted with all kinds of points of view.

In *The Young Bird*, an ignorant young bird Amalia flies over a landscape full of puzzling images ('doodles'), wondering what the things are that she is looking at from above. Poor Amalia herself eventually ends up as one of the mysterious objects on the ground, a topic of discussion amongst the other birds.

In *The Dachshund's Very End*, a dachshund is so long that, although he can see his tail at the other side of the page, he can't get close to it. When

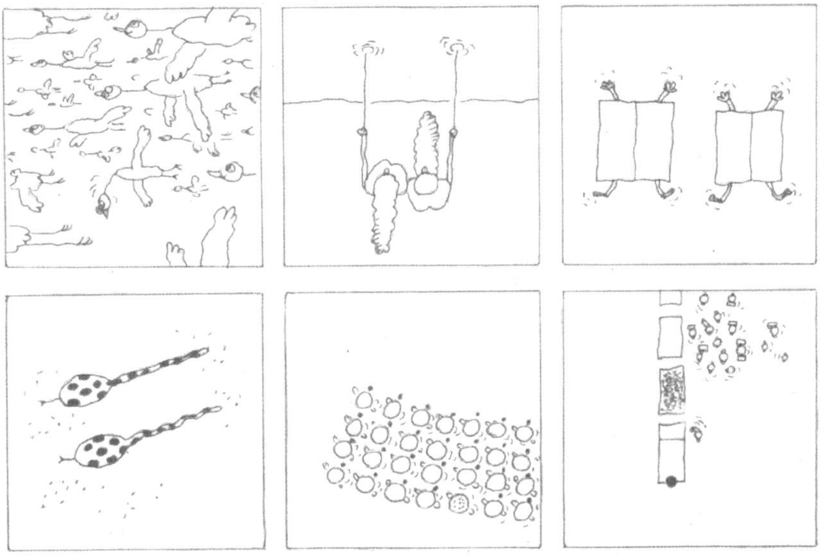

Fiddle Fumble Stories: The Young Bird.

he and two of his friends decide to walk over to find out why this is, the outcome is quite different from his expectations.

The Little Dog tells the story of a dog who, put outside on a dark Christmas night, follows many different light sources along its journey, and is finally guided by a strong light from above to a nice, warm stable.

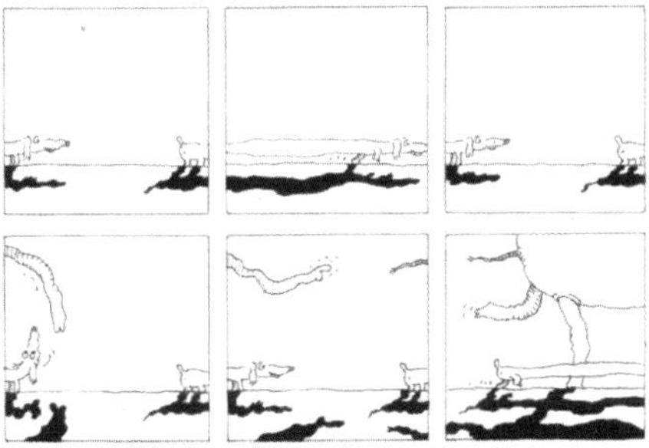

Fiddle Fumble Stories: The Dachshund's Very End.

Fiddle Fumble Stories: The Little Dog.

Recently I wrote and illustrated five new Fiddle Fumble stories, this time with the illustrations in colour. There is a story about a blind mole who bumps into an old canon who sends his new friend off to the promise of vision; another story explains the hazards faced by a young monkey who suffers from vertigo; and another one tells us why the chicken crossed the road. Like the previous Fiddle Fumble narratives, all stories deal with visual ideas, offering young readers a different point of view of reality. Les 400 Coups has since folded, so I'm still looking for a publisher to take it on.

Fiddle Fumble Stories: The Old Canon and the Mole.

Fiddle Fumble Stories: The Monkey who was afraid of Heights.

Fiddle Fumble Stories: Why the Chicken crossed the Road.

In 2005, a good friend of mine, Paul Nieuwenhuis, died of the disease of Kahler, a cancer which affects the bone-marrow. Paul and his wife Janneke had a large house in a very nice area of The Hague where I always stayed when passing through Holland on my way from Montreal to Kassel.

In a strange way I felt somewhat responsible for his death. A few years before Paul was diagnosed, on a weekend in winter when I happened to sleep over at their place, I woke up early Sunday morning, looked out the window and saw that it was one of those beautiful winter days perfect for skating. I jumped out of bed and almost dragged Paul, who was not an early riser, to the polder nearby where other early skaters were already gliding over the many canals criss-crossing the fields.

Paul and I put on our skates and took off, but it was early winter, the ice was still thin and about one kilometer after our start Paul crashed through the ice. The canal wasn't very deep so Paul hoisted himself onto the side and after he'd put his skates back on, we continued our trip, like any Dutch skater would have done. However, during the rest of our expedition, Paul's feet stayed wet and a week later he caught a cold. It wasn't a bad cold, but it just didn't go away. Finally, Paul consulted a doctor who diagnosed him with something much more serious than a cold, the disease of Kahler.

The disease wasn't, of course, caused by skating with wet feet. Paul was already infected with Kahler before our trip and in a way, he was lucky that it was detected quite early on by his cold. After many years of fighting the cancer, Paul finally succumbed and sadly died in December 2005.

Inspired by the way I remembered him (for instance, Paul often made jokes about language), I sent a couple of semi-funny/sad cartoons to Janneke who used one of my drawings as the obituary notice for his passing.

Paul's card was the first of many more of those funny/sad cartoons I designed (although I'm not sure that they were always appreciated by the surviving relatives).

Design for my friend Paul's obituary (his typical 'au réservoir' instead of the French 'au revoir').

Design for our artist friend Pierrot who made beautiful moving sculptures from various mechanical parts. St. Peter is saying "Good Lord, me, fed up with computers and look who shows up?"

Design for friend, animator and musician Rosto with his 'Mephisto' looks.

Design for Jacques, a friend and animator, who was known for his animation on the pin-screen.

I retired from my Kassel teaching job in 2005. I was 65 years old, the age that the German state pensioned off their employees. I felt it was time for me to go anyway; I was an old school animator and students made more and more use of computer-generated images, a technique I had not much affinity with.

Thomas Meyer-Hermann and Andreas Hykade, two excellent filmmakers from Stuttgart, were appointed as the new joint animation professors at the Kassel University.

My students organized a great farewell party at a local cinema with films (theirs and mine) and speeches. The event was a very animated, and for me, a touching finale to my teaching career.

Although the Kassel job had been quite rewarding, I had never felt entirely comfortable as a teacher, and I was happy to be able to go back to full-time filmmaking.

REFLECTIONS ON THE CRAFT

After my retirement from Kassel, I made many more films, but two of them are particularly worth mentioning because of their typical use of narrative space in storytelling.

The first one I'd like to expand on a little is called *Oedipus*, with a story which isn't told forwards, from A to Z, but backwards, from Z to A. To help people understand that the end of the story starts at the beginning, I chose the legend of Oedipus, which, as most people know, ends badly: Oedipus unknowingly kills his father and then marries his mother.

The first sequence of the film, a very short overview of the murder and the subsequent love affair between Oedipus and his mother, is animated forwards. The rest of the film, in which Oedipus is trying to understand why the woman he loves seems suddenly very upset by a little trick he shows her (by which she recognizes who he is), is animated backwards.

The backward animation documents how the lives of Oedipus and his parents unfolded, all the way to the end when Oedipus is born from the womb of the woman he is now married to. Grasping the awful truth of who she is, he exclaims: 'She's my mother!' End of film.

In order for the audience to catch up with Oedipus' ongoing quest to figure out who he is, he visits at regular intervals a group therapy session of a variety of cartoon characters I borrowed from well-known Film Board films. The characters I had chosen had, as often happens in animation, their own problems: the protagonist from Cordell Barker's *The-Cat-Came-Back* is haunted by the unrelenting returning cat; everyone from Chris Hinton's *Blackfly* is pestered by terrible little flies; the postman from John Weldon's *Special Delivery* is dead (not much animation needed); Bob from *Bob's Birthday* is vainly trying to hide his nakedness; the wife from *Big Snit* is bothered by the outcome of her Scrabble letters; and Marv Newland's three-headed character has the obvious problem of trying to make unified decisions.

Oedipus *in his therapy session with other National Film Board characters.*

During all this random action a bewildered Oedipus tries to find out what's wrong with him.

One of the problems I encountered when designing the characters was how to make Oedipus recognizable as the son of his father. I decided to give them both the ability to take off their heads. Thus, when Oedipus, sitting next to his mother in bed, takes off his head to go to sleep, the mother, seeing that the young man can do the same trick as her murdered husband (who's lifeless head is sitting on the night table), realizes that the two must be related. Although I was aware that the disposable-head feature made the story more complicated for an unprepared audience, at the same time it was a fun component to play with.

The Oedipus *murder scene, his father's snoring headsets on the night table.*

Oedipus was a film in which I also experimented with my drawing style. Although I'm able to draw straight lines, I usually employ wiggly lines in my animation. But in the case of the Oedipus visuals, I also fooled around with volume and dimensions; at random I made characters fatter or thinner during their movement, sometimes rendering them to a mere line or a pair of eyes while moving about. It was very satisfying to find out how forgiving animation is, how far you can go, how the eye easily follows the progression of the subject throughout its movement.

The music-track, created by Judith Gruber-Stitzer, has a slightly backward feel to it and flows nicely with the reverting visuals. I remember that some of the musicians hired to play had a hard time understanding the complexity of Judith's music. Judith who masters all kinds of instruments, often had to step in and play parts of the score herself.

Then there was the voice of Oedipus, talking to himself when going back in time and, on occasion, speaking to his fellow patients when looking for answers during the group sessions. Amongst the many actors we cast for the role we found a talented young actor of Romanian origin, Alexander Ivanovici, who came up with a rambling voice which was perfect for the confused Oedipus character. During the voice recording Alexander often took off by himself, creating some kind of crazy monologue. When the credits came up at the end of the film, Alexander didn't stop his narrative but carried on with some nonsensical prattle of his own invention and because it was so funny, we kept it in. After recording the English version, the perfectly bilingual actor improvised a similar wacky discourse in French.

Whenever I watch the film again, I always look forward to the end-credits, enjoying the absurd improvisations of Alexander's Oedipus, who, finally wise to the facts, is trying to come to terms with the discovery of his origin.

The last film I made at the National Film Board of Canada before moving to France was a multiscreen project called *Cat meets Dog*. Like my film *Oedipus*, it was coproduced by the Dutch ilLuster studios.

Inspired by the 'animal chase' movies of the fifties and sixties, I'd always wanted to make a dog-chasing-cat film myself. Using anthropomorphic animals as characters was new to me. Somehow there was never the need to replace my human cartoon characters with animals.

Since I had made quite a few films in which the screen was divided in various parts as a story device, I knew about the pitfalls of creating too

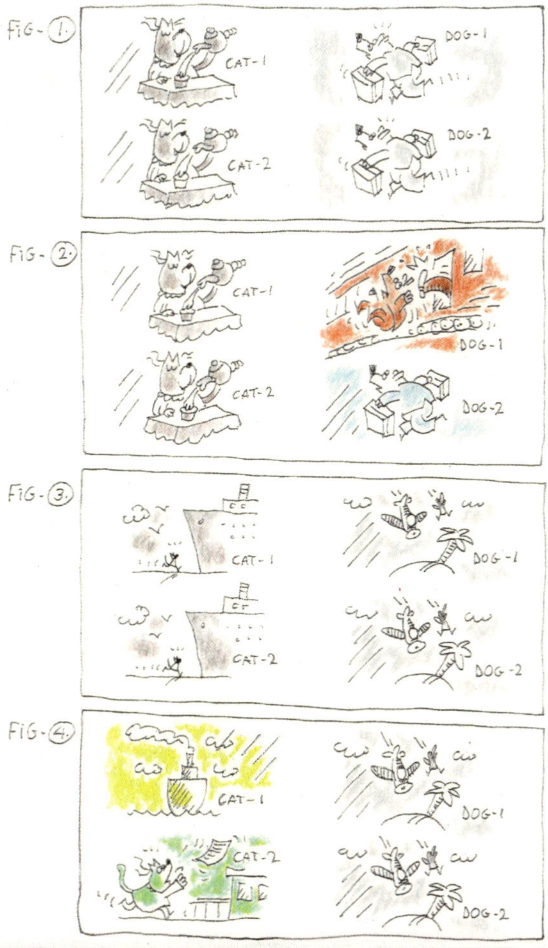

Storyboard panels from Cat meets Dog. *The coloured frames are where the action takes place.*

much confusion for an audience trying to understand the nature of my presentation. If the arrangement on screen is too complicated, the viewer, not knowing where to look, might give up following the story. In *Cat meets Dog* I tried to make it easy for the spectator by consistently animating only the action of one of the two protagonists, either the cat or the dog, in two of the four panels attributed to them, while 'freezing' the other panels. By guiding the viewer from one side of the screen to the other through the animation, the film tells the story of how the two protagonists, one a cat, the other a dog, receive an amorous looking invitation to a romantic meeting.

Although both the cat and the dog appear to already be in relationships, they seem unable to resist the attraction of the invitation and slip away from their respective homes. From the way the story is constructed it seems that when the cat and the dog set out on their adventure, they are destined to meet, heading for an adulterous rendezvous in Paris. After overcoming many obstacles, the two protagonists almost meet. However, in the end it's not them, but their abandoned partners who run into each other, an encounter of the cat and dog species which reveals their true natures.

When setting up the story I made a list of the contrasting characteristics of the protagonists: the female cat being careful and orderly; the male dog being impulsive and sloppy. These notes helped me to come up with ideas for the obstacles which each of them encountered on their way to the meeting. During most of the film the anthropomorphic characters were decently dressed and comported themselves quite civilly. But when at a certain point in the film they took off their clothes, their manners fell away, and they briefly bounced back to being cats and dogs with an innate dislike of each other.

☆ ☆ ☆

Over the years I have frequented many festivals with my films. On the occasions when I didn't have a film in competition, I was often asked to be on the festivals' juries. It was a job I really enjoyed. One of the reasons I liked being on juries was that it helped me to focus on the films presented for us to judge. Observing what is happening around me doesn't come naturally to me; I live very often in my head, thinking about things that have very little to do with what's in front of me. Consequently, my ideas for films are never really based on observations of occurrences happening near me, they're almost always figments of my imagination.

When on a jury, I had to force myself to concentrate on the films, to make notes, making sure to remember all the details of the films to be discussed later with the other jury members.

Juries would sometimes make the wrong decisions, of course, but when that happened and I was part of it, the responsibility always weighed heavily on me. I remember two or three occasions when we clearly made bad decisions, voting for the wrong films, bad judgements which haunted me for many years.

Fortunately, being on juries was mostly a pleasant experience. I often made friends with the other members and there was usually very little disagreement amongst us. Watching and analyzing animation is an interesting occupation. It helps you to understand how other people approach this complex art form.

When I got older, I often functioned as jury president. Once, in this capacity, during the farewell dinner of the 2009 Tehran Animation Film Festival in Iran, I was given an enormous stone relief sculpture as a thank-you gift for my contribution to the festival. Realizing that I could never bring such a large, sculpted plaque with me on the plane, I asked the organization to send it to an address in Holland where my daughter and her two young children lived. The festival granted my wish, and upon its arrival in Holland, my grandchildren took out their paintbrushes and turned the massive sculpture into a colourful artwork of their own. They painted the noses of the people seated in the scenery red, added colourful flowers to their robes and converted the barren ground into a fresh green polder. I'm sure the old Persians would have agreed to the transformation.

It was actually my second visit to the Tehran Film Festival. The first was in 1979, when as a young animator I was invited to the festival with one of my earlier films. This was during the period when the Shah and his family had already fled Iran and Ayatollah Khomeini had not yet returned from France as the country's new leader.

It was certainly an interesting but not a very pleasant experience; there was such a difference in the distribution of wealth amongst the rich and the rest of the population. For instance, being offered free first-class flights in almost empty jumbo jets to extravagant thousand-and-one-night-like festival parties in Shiraz and Isfahan felt quite embarrassing to someone who came from countries where equality amongst citizens was more the norm than the exception.

☆ ☆ ☆

In 2009, when a newly approved law granted Dutch natives dual citizenship, I turned my Canadian 'landed Immigrant' status into a much-desired Canadian citizenship. I no longer had to worry about limited time abroad and would always be able to go back to the country in which I spent much of the most memorable years of my adult life.

For independent animators of short artistic films, it was never easy to make a living. We almost always depended on subsidies from the country where we resided, not a source of income easy to come by. Therefore, in my position, having two citizenships proved to be very convenient; I could ask for my projects to be subsidized in Canada, in Holland and, the Netherlands being part of the EU, many other European countries as well.

Getting older, the long and severe Canadian winters made living in Montreal less enjoyable. Montreal had always been a fun city with a lot of activities, but in winter, the snow and ice made the streets difficult to navigate. Also, having to dress up warmly to beat the cold, for instance for waiting in line for a restaurant or theatre, turned the decision of whether to go out more and more to a decision to stay home.

In spring, summer and fall, I always went to the National Film Board on my bicycle. But when the winter approached and a possible first snowstorm was announced on the morning's newscast, I still remember the odd feeling of excitement, taking out my bike and cycling to my office, a ride of about 40 minutes. Then, later in the day, I would look out of the window and when I would see the first indication of a blizzard, I would quickly pack up, jump on my bike and start cycling back home. It was always too late to ride all the way; usually after about ten minutes into the storm I had to lift my bike onto my shoulder and fight my way back through the icy winds and growing snowbanks.

Photo: Diane Dauphinais

Our Montreal street in winter.

In winter I loved to go cross-country skiing with friends in the beautiful hills of the Laurentians, about two hours drive from Montreal. But as we got older, most of us felt less and less inclined to first drive for a few hours over slippery roads, and then hurl ourselves down the slopes with the risk of smashing into trees, an activity quite challenging for our now brittle bones.

Diane and I decided to move to the south of France, where the only danger of colliding with trees was not paying attention when driving down the scenic Routes Nationales, lined with large shade-providing plane trees. Like many northern Europeans, I had always cherished a secret desire to live in this beautiful country and when I married Diane, who, like many Canadians was curious about her roots, we started to explore the land of her ancestors.

We ended up moving into a very nice old *maison de maître* in Olargues, a picturesque ancient village in the south of the country. We kept our residence in Montreal for the time being. First of all, because we loved the city, it was always fun to be back and enjoy

Photo: Diane Dauphinais

The garden behind our house in Olargues.

our old stomping grounds; but also, although our big stone house in southern France was lovely and cool in summer, in winter we couldn't really get the place sufficiently warm. As Canadians, we were spoiled by very well-heated homes when it got chilly.

Photo: Paul Driessen

Diane decorating the old maison de maître in Olargues.

Nonetheless, a few years later, it was time to make a change. One of the main reasons for me was that the National Film Board of Canada appeared to be less and less interested in my ideas for films. I guess they felt that they had sponsored enough Paul Driessen films and would rather support young filmmakers instead. I couldn't blame them, of course, but the idea of spending the long Montreal winters at home without much to do didn't appeal to me. France, however, did show interest in my new projects, and we decided to leave Montreal and settle permanently in France.

My cartoon about National Film Board producer David Verrall being uninterested in my new projects.

Our plan was to sell both our residence in Montreal and the old house in Olargues and with the money build ourselves a new modern home in France. We found a piece of land on a hill with a magnificent view not far from our old village, and started to design plans for a new comfortable contemporary house with studio space for both Diane and myself.

We were eager to start the construction, but we ran into difficulties selling the house in Olargues. Although it was a lovely place with a big garden in the back, the house was quite close to a small but busy Route Nationale, where, especially during the summer season, many cars were passing through. Eventually, we found potential buyers, an English couple who wanted to relocate to France. They loved the property and were ready to move in but had to resolve some financial issues at home first before we could close the deal.

The Jeffreys eventually bought our house, but it took a long time to get their finances in order. (The A-9 is a big highway in France).

During this dilemma our very generous Dutch friends Loes & Arne offered to help us out, to tide us over during the time we needed to build our dream house. To keep them happy until we could pay them back, I sent them very many cartoons:

Loes & Arne cartoon about whether an exchange would be alright for paying back our loan.

Paul asking for more money.

'You know, construction on a hill is very different from building in Holland'.

'Well, at the same time we added some buildings to accommodate our foreign guests'.

Loes & Arne trying to get their money back from Diane's Canadian relatives.

Loes & Arne after losing all their money: 'Nice letter from Paul, very cozy house, he says'.

To pull off our plan to build a modern house in the national park of the Languedoc, the region where we lived, we had to overcome quite a few obstacles. The park was a protected area, and we were submitted to many regulations. Fortunately, we had a builder, a maître d'oeuvre named Jean-Louis Ehl, who knew all the ins and outs and who was able to convince the authorities to accept most of our ideas.

We had also some sloppy sub-contractors, one of whom started digging the hole for the foundation at the wrong place. Little Jean-Louis stepped in just in time and although he almost got into a fistfight with the bulgy man in charge (Diane separated the two) the hole was filled up and a new one made at the proper place.

"No, no, wrong place again, not in the road".

Although the drawings of the ground plan were well-executed, we were often puzzled by what was what. Fortunately, our *maître d'oeuvre* always helped out. If it wasn't for Jean-Louis, I have my doubts if we ever would have been able to get our house built the way we wanted. Jean-Louis on the other hand, was a bit puzzled by my sense of humour.

"Oh, hello Jean-Louis; you know, Paul was never good at straight lines." (I'm known for my wiggly lines in animation).

Since building a house was the first time for both of us, we had a hard time estimating heights and surfaces. The architect who had designed the original plan was a hands-on person and didn't use the computer programs where one could see the proportions of the various components compared to the size of the inhabitants inside. Instead, he had built a small maquette out of cardboard, quite nice to look at but not very effective for assessing space and people.

Although we had to give in to some of the building regulations, in the end our new home was quite close to the house we had in mind. It was covered in wood which gave it a Canadian touch and it had a zinc roof instead of the traditional roof tiles which rattle in the strong winds, a frequent occurrence in our region. Most importantly, the house was very comfortable, both cool in summer (good insulation) and warm in winter (floor heating). And, of course, it had a beautiful view of its surroundings:

"Zut, as a Canadian I always had problems with the difference between inches and centimeters".

"Oh oh, I held the plan upside-down".

the green oak forest in the back; small vineyards protected by hills in front; and the spectacular ravine of the 'Gorge d'Héric' on the North side.

One of the difficulties I had to cope with when moving to a small village in the south of France was that I was deprived of the technical support I had always heavily leaned upon when working at the National Film Board in Canada and its animation community.

Photo: Diane Dauphinais

The view from the kitchen under construction of the 'Gorge d'Héric'

When we moved to the area where we decided to settle, I had already done some research to find out if there were animation studios not too far away that I could possibly turn to for emergencies. Through our good friend and fellow artist Isabelle Landmann, I was introduced to the Praxinos studios in Montpellier, about a two-hour drive from our house. I also found out that the French animator Jean-François Laguionie (who had won the Grand Prix at my very first Annecy festival) had founded 'La Fabrique', a studio in the nearby hills of Saint-Laurent-le-Miniers.

The most urgent problem I had to solve, however, was how to go about shooting my line tests. I couldn't jump in my car for a two-hour drive every time I wanted to test the movement of my animation. Shortly before leaving Canada, my colleague Randall Finnerty, one of the many very helpful people at the National Film Board, had tried to get me acquainted with the Cintiq, a tablet most animators used for shooting their films and line tests. I always was a slow pupil when things didn't really interest me much and never succeeded in getting the device under control.

Fortunately, another National Film Board friend, Janet Perlman, who was familiar with all kinds of computer animation programs, offered to help me. Over the following weeks, she patiently forwarded me instructions over the internet, explaining how to set up a computer line-test program to shoot paper-drawn animation in my studio in France.

Actually, the most important factor that made me feel at ease with both my work and my life in this new and somewhat isolated location, was that I had married Diane. She was not only perfectly comfortable with the language of the country we had moved to, but due to her proficiency in practical matters such as construction, computer techniques and her medical skills, I felt very confident planning to build a new house from scratch, setting up my studio which heavily depended on good internet connections, and continuing to ride my bike with the knowledge that Diane would always be able to fix me up when I would have one of my unfortunate tumbles.

Besides, Diane was an inspiring artist and an excellent photographer. Since my memory was never my greatest asset, I'm very fortunate to have an abundance of pictures Diane took over the years to remind me of the eventful years we have shared.

Despite my early fascination with comic books, like *Tintin* and *Lucky Luke,* I never developed much enthusiasm for the graphic novel. That lack of interest changed when I discovered the vigorous drawing style of Johan De Moor, who, together with the writer Desberg, created *La Vache.*

La Vache, a cow, a common grazer amidst other farm animals, gets up on her hind legs, when an emergency arises, dresses up in a raincoat and a felt hat and, as a very astute detective, saves the world from terrible disasters. When her mission is accomplished, she sheds her clothing and turns back to being an ordinary cow.

What's interesting about De Moor's design is that between his drawings of La Vache on the warpath, he inserts all kinds of pictures that are not his, often old book illustrations which appear to be from another era.

My inserts were short interruptions of the main happenings, in which a detail of the main action (which was, at this point, frozen on the screen) was placed inside a small square frame and told a very brief funny story, unrelated to the scene it had been taken from. The square then pops out again, and the main storyline resumes.

This was a film in which quite a few narrative space ideas were introduced. Death arrives as a 3D character in a

This concept reminded me of the little inserts I added to a couple of scenes in Death and the Writer, *a film set in the Middle Ages, which I had made in the late 80s.*

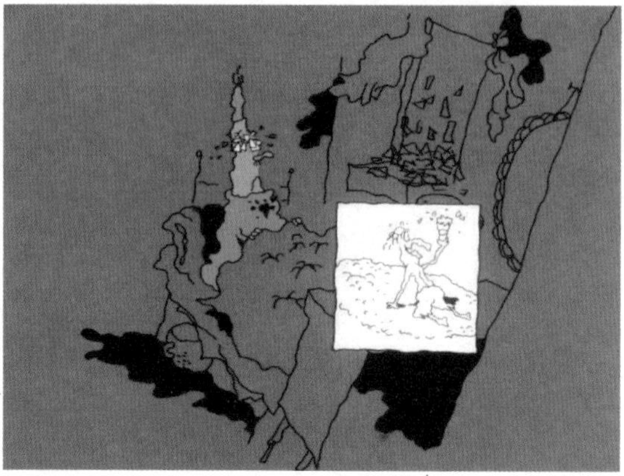

This concept reminded me of the little inserts I added to a couple of scenes in Death and the Writer, *a film set in the Middle Ages, which I had made in the late 80s.*

small town. The town and its occupants are drawn on a 2D level, so Death can be seen walking on top of the animated events happening in the town. When he spots someone to his liking, Death touches his target lightly with his scythe, causing his victim to expire.

However, at the end of the film we come to realize that none of what we have seen so far is real; it's a running account of an old archivist documenting the history of his time on the blank pages of his book. While he often succeeds in scratching out the havoc Death's actions cause, in the end Death jumps on top of the page in which the Writer himself is depicted,

Death jumps on top of the level in which the Writer is depicted.

which, turning over, appears as a line. Bringing his scythe lightly down on the spot where the Writer is situated, Death ends the story.

Death always played an important part in my films, not so much because I'm bothered by the phenomenon itself, but because of its finality, it makes a good ending to a story. And in the Middle Ages, Death was a frequent visitor in many of its stories and images and, represented by a skeleton, appeared to be an interesting icon for animation.

When we moved to France, I discovered some other very charming comic book artists: Benjamin Renner and his *Grand Méchant Renard,* Jacques Azam and his *Mandarine & Co* and *Winshluss,* my favourite French illustrator and *bande dessinée* artist, who applies different drawing styles to his whimsical and often morbid scenarios. Winshluss did great and twisted renditions of the Bible and of Pinocchio, the little wooden boy turning bad. In Winshluss' portrayal, Pinocchio is a metal puppet who is constructed by an evil inventor, at first seduced by his creator's wife, then sold to the military as a weapon.

Like Winshluss, I also often take inspiration from fairytales and biblical stories. It saves a lot of time (and drawings) when you don't have to introduce your character and explain his or her motivations in the story you're going to tell.

In my early comic strip *Jonas,* I used a theme from the Bible (Jonah and the Whale), a story everybody is familiar with. We all take for granted that a person named Jonas might end up in a whale. In my strip, the leader of a bunch of nomadic people is trapped inside a big snake. Loyal to their chief, the group, of which Jonas is a member, decides to settle down and look for accommodation similar to their leader's habitat, choosing large animals for living quarters. After many adventures, Jonas befriends a whale who agrees to let him move in.

Jonas, ending up in a dwelling of his liking.

In my films there are also lots of settings referring to universal tales and facts. An early film of mine, *David*, obviously alludes to David from the

Old Testament, known for being small. I used him again, disguised as one of the seven dwarves facing Goliath in my film *3 Misses*.

3 Misses was crammed with references to popular narrative: Little Red Riding Hood, Sleeping Beauty, Snow White, (confused princes, ladies in distress, cowboy shoot-outs).

Still from 3 Misses, *the Dwarf facing Goliath.*

Fairytale panels, 3 Misses *storyboard.*

Like the Canadians before, the French were very good to me. They knew my work through my many visits to the animation festival of Annecy and I was also one of the founding members (in name only) of the animation studio 'Folimage' in Valence, to which they later added 'La Poudrière', now a prominent animation school where I have frequently been invited to give workshops.

France has many excellent schools for film and animation and there are many film festivals which are very popular both amongst film professionals and students. One of those festivals is in Angers, in the north of France, not far from the city of Angoulême where a famous school for comics and animation is located. In the early days of our permanent settling in France, I was asked to be on one of the juries of this yearly festival called 'Festival Premiers Plans'. It's a festival where they present first films (live action features, shorts, and animation) of the new generation of filmmakers, mainly from France, but also some from other European countries.

It's a popular festival and tons of people show up; there are conferences with professionals and well-known actors, lively exchanges amongst filmmakers, as well as many interviews with people of various motion picture disciplines. I was invited to be interviewed on stage with Xavier Kawa-Topor, an erudite historian of animation and the director of the illustrious Residency of Fontevraud, a beautiful old abbey (where Richard the Lionheart and his mother Eleanore of Aquitaine are entombed), a meeting place very popular amongst animation aficionados.

During the interview the last question Xavier posed to me was: 'since you live here, how come you've never made a film in France?' I answered him that I would have loved to but that I had never been asked. When the interview was over, I was approached by Emmanuel-Alain Raynal who, together with his partner Pierre Baussaron, runs the successful animation production studio 'Miyu' in Paris. Emmanuel said that he would be very interested to work with me and asked me to come up with ideas for a short, animated film.

Soon after, we met again, and I showed him a couple of concepts I had for potential films. We agreed on a seven-minute project called *The Two Shoes,* an idea based on one of my Fiddle Fumble Stories. It's a tale of two shoes, worn by four generations of individuals. The shoes grow old during the process and eventually decide to stick with the last person they end up with, an old man, whom they follow into his grave.

Poster for The 2 Shoes.

We had a lot of delays while making the film because early on in the production, Covid struck. Since I worked at home, I quietly continued with the animation, but during the postproduction of the film it became more and more difficult to stick to arrangements and get things done.

One plan was to ask Chaim Tannenbaum, a singer from Montreal, to sing the ballad we had programmed for the film. Chaim has a beautiful somewhat fragile tenor voice and I had often heard him sing with the acclaimed McGarrigle sisters. While working on the lyrics of the ballad I had asked Judith Gruber-Stitzer to write the music for the tragic story of the Shoes. Chaim, in the meantime, had moved to New York, and when the Covid epidemic became a worldwide threat, he was not allowed to cross the border and couldn't return to Canada for the recording.

Judith therefore, dropped the sorrowful ballad idea and wrote an entirely new music score for a different kind of voice. Having spent my childhood years in Moscow, I had always loved the sound of the Russian language and with the help of the Montreal Russian community, we wrote a new song with Russian lyrics, sung by a local folksinger.

The protagonists in the film, the two shoes, are passed on from one generation to the next through four individuals: the first one is a child who comes across the shoes in the forest. He puts them on but then loses them at a dwelling where a closed door blocks his escape from a hungry bear. Subsequently a young adult spots the two shoes left behind at his doorstep. He puts them on but when he takes them off again at the side of a river he is trying to cross, the young man doesn't come back to claim them. Then a middle-aged man, whose clothes are stolen, finds the shoes at the riverbank. He puts them on, but they slip from his feet after an unfortunate fall from his window. Finally, the shoes are retrieved by an old man who, like in the book, takes the now old and worn shoes to his grave.

I had written the tale of *The Two Shoes* in my Fiddle Fumble Stories from the point of view of the shoes themselves. In the book they talk to each other, discussing whether being passed on from one person to the next might be to their advantage or not. In the film there is no spoken word. To enhance the visual drama, I gave the shoes a submissive role; the shoes are

Four illustrations of the generation sequences of The Two Shoes.

the passive transmitters of bad luck, unbeknownst to the characters who put them on.

Curiously, it was not so long ago that I realized that using a unique point of view was a hallmark of many of my films:

- In *David*, it's David himself who, from his point of view, explains how, as a very small person, he is threatened by the many dangers of the very large and inattentive world.
- In *Elbowing*, the dissident individual outsmarts the establishment by having a different view of his surroundings.
- In *The Killing of an Egg*, the protagonist discovers, to his and the spectator's surprise, that he is stuck in the same place as the one he destroyed.
- In *Sunny side up*, the audience, like the castaway on his island, is put to the test about what's up and what's down.
- *In 2D or not 2D*, we jump from three-dimensions to two-dimensions to one dimension, spaces occupied by characters invisible to each other.
- In *Oedipus* the protagonist is only able to understand his fate by going backwards in time.
- In *Cat meets Dog* the film is constructed to set the spectator on the wrong foot from the very beginning.

Fly for One Day was a project designed for the Imax screen about small versus big and how different realities sense the passage of time. As shown in animated images, the perception of time is relative—humans move very slowly in comparison to flies. Although an interesting POV idea, the film was never made.

As a final example, one of my last films, *The Origin of Sound*, reverses the cinematic order of visuals and sound. The Origin of Sound is a film about the creation of the world in which most of the visuals are already concocted, but sound doesn't yet exist.

Co-directed by the Belgian stop-motion specialist, Toon Loenders, it's the story of an omnipotent sound engineer, in the film an unpleasant pixelated individual, who is looking for sound effects to go along with the action of the two puppet-like characters he is manipulating, Man and Woman, both of them also pixelated.

Since sound doesn't exist yet, the Soundman combs through his collection of animated cartoons, which are all supplied with Foley soundtracks, to find the appropriate sound he wants to synchronise with the movements of the two characters. The cartoons in the Soundman's collection are all quite distasteful but he seems to feel that the sound effects he extracts from them fit nicely with the sounds he is looking for, linking them to the basic actions to which he submits his subjects.

Storyboard 9, Tub Turd.
The sound needed was the 'drip drip' of drops falling into a porridge-like substance.

Storyboard 11, Dumbo.
The sound needed was a big 'Slosh' sound of a bucket with slimy content being emptied.

Storyboard 20, Drop Pants.
The sound needed was a 'Boink' and a crunchy 'Snap' sound.

Storyboard 22, Deep Throat.
The sound needed was the 'Plock' sound of chopping through soft material on wood.

Excited by the results he's getting, the Soundman exposes his two victims to more and more unpleasantries. In the end, however, when they feel that the Soundman has gone too far, the puppet-like Man and Woman revolt, leading to the Soundman's downfall.

The film was a coproduction between The Netherlands (ilLuster) and Belgium (S.O.I.L. Geert van Goethem) and although it was not an easy project to get financed, we secured Dutch and Flemish film funding.

The challenge and fun for me was to come up with a series of 'dirty' cartoons which would produce the appropriate sound effects needed to accompany the action of the man and the woman. Within quite a short time I wrote a succession of twenty-nine storyboards, all with the same distasteful quality. A few weeks later, however, when I tried to think of some more of the same, I appeared to have lost the inspiration and wasn't really able to reach the same 'heights' of funny dirty cartoon stories.

The twenty-nine story ideas which were used for The Origin of Sound.

I'm one of the few fortunate people who, as far as I remember, never really suffered from 'writer's block', but this confronting experience, strange as it may seem, made me aware of the fragilities of the creative mind.

It was interesting for me to be present at screenings of this rather distasteful film. Audiences, confronted by the improper jokes, at first would grow silent, then, when people began to understand what the film was about, some would start to laugh, inspiring others to join them.

I also learned that the kind of humour I was trying to convey was to a certain extent culture-based. While Anglophone communities often seemed to label the cartoons of the film as cheap fun for adolescents, the Dutch, Belgians, Germans, and French appeared to appreciate the broad aspect of the humour and weren't ashamed of openly enjoying the absurdity of my ideas.

I quite delight in these cartoons by Hurzlmeier, Vuillemin and Gummbah. One might find them borderline distasteful, but they are very inspiring to me and illustrate my own taste in the genre.

Rattelsneck, Germany: 'Sorry, one of your breasts is hanging out';
'Oh my God, I forgot my baby in the bus'.

Vuillemin, France: 'Remember when we were young and wanted to look like Brigitte Bardot?';
'Yes, so what?' 'Well, we've finally succeeded.'

Gummbah, Netherlands: 'Don't freak out'.

Since I've seen and appreciated very many cartoons from all of these different cultures and countries during my life, I recognized the reaction of the various audiences. When attending an *Origin of Sound* screening, I would be relieved when audiences started to laugh, but I would suffer through it when the reaction was less favourable.

In March 2020, when I turned 80, I was invited by the Dutch Directors Guild to receive their prestigious Oeuvre Award. The Dutch Directors Guild awards ceremony is a yearly event in Amsterdam where filmmakers excelling in various categories receive awards. It's a big party with food, drinks and entertainment with more than 200 people attending.

But March 2020 was when the Corona virus started to rear its ugly head and just as Diane and I were about to board the train to Amsterdam the Dutch prime minister came on the radio and announced that all gatherings of over fifty people were to be cancelled. We phoned the organisers who were in tears but said that nothing could be done about it, we had to sit it out till better times.

In the same week I had also planned a celebratory lunch at a very nice restaurant in a rose garden in The Hague with my whole family—my children, grandchildren, brother, sister and cousins with their partners—to salute this respectable age. However, after consulting with some of the more vulnerable family members, we agreed that we also should postpone this festivity to a later date, hoping that the elderly amongst us would still be alive. (Unfortunately, when we did hold the lunch two years later, one of my older cousins had died.)

My old producers, Nico Crama and Willem Thijssen, both of great importance for the development of the Dutch animated short.

Another event, a presentation of a selection of films from my producer friend Nico Crama and myself at the EYE film museum in Amsterdam, was also cancelled. It was to commemorate Nico's 85th birthday and my 80th, delicate ages. Fortunately, both Nico and I survived, and the occasion was repeated when Covid wasn't such a danger anymore.

Growing older as an artist who has always been very productive has two sides to it. Although my reputation may have been growing a bit stale lately, my films being less in demand than before, whenever I approach the various institutions who sponsor animated shorts with new ideas, I don't doubt that they'll consider my submissions seriously. However, the committees who consider the new projects tend to compare my new proposals with my previous films, making sure that the new idea is a step forward, not a repetition of what I've done before.

An additional problem is that my film ideas have become more and more complex and are harder to understand. Most animators write linear stories for their films; they present a storyboard, a series of successive pictures with accompanying text, which is easy to read.

I always struggle with my presentations; how, for instance, do you create a storyboard which explains a split-screen or multi-screen idea, a visualization of a multitude of panels which all have references to each other in the progression of the story, but no proper connections which read from left to right. Or how can you fabricate a storyboard that the eye scans from left to right of a story which goes backwards—from right to left?

At the time of writing, I'm still trying to get *Prumf* off the ground, a project which I think might turn out to be one of my most interesting films. *Prumf* started out as a birth announcement for Kaj, one of my grandsons, a drawing full of 'frozen' little stories. Many years later (little Kaj is now 17, and is six feet tall) I picked it up again and saw the potential for making this compilation of very playful illustrations into a film.

Little Kaj's birth announcement, the inspiration for Prumf.

My idea is not to animate all the images on screen at the same time but to convert the individual illustrations into very short absurdist stories and then bring each one of them separately to life. At first sight, the stories don't seem to have much in common except for the unconventional storytelling. At a certain point in the film, however, the audience will realize that links are made either through sound or the subject matter, a process full of surprises.

The leading thread running through the film is the concept of 'disinformation'. It's about how the application of sound can influence the image. Each one of the vignettes is accompanied by sound effects which tell a slightly different story than the visuals seem to convey. While watching the images come to life the sound will increasingly thwart the audience's understanding of what is taking place on screen.

I replaced the original design with three different compositions, three sequences, each one containing six to eight vignettes in monochrome colours, quite a few of them borrowed from Kaj's original birth announcement. I then proceeded to write a variety of 'sound stories' to accompany all these individual snapshots which, each in turn, would switch to colour and come to life.

The sound stories were all very carefully planned and written down in detail. The idea was, and still is, to discuss them with a sound engineer who will not just implement the ideas I'll present to him but who might also add his own suggestions. Unlike the animation, this portion of the film is open to improvisation. As far as the abstract components like music and sound in film are concerned, I always love to get creative professionals involved.

Prumf is one of those projects which is hard to describe in text and images. It doesn't have a linear story and the importance of sound, an abstract component, is very difficult to put in words at the storyboard stage.

The first sequence of Prumf, *the film.*

The second sequence of Prumf, *the film.*

The third sequence of Prumf, *the film.*

Again, my Belgian friend and producer Geert van Goethem saw its potential and with his help I'm now composing a proposal which I hope that the Flemish and Dutch Film Fund will understand.

Since I'm getting quite old and time is running out, I tend to start the animation of new projects I believe in before any financial agreement is in place. In case of *Prumf*, I kicked off about two years ago with some animated tests, then, as I saw the allure of the project, I began to animate one vignette after the other and, while waiting for the outcome of the various committees discussing the proposal, I have now almost finished the whole film. Close to twelve minutes of animation is sitting in boxes, waiting to be scanned, composited, coloured and then sent to the sound studio, where it all is supposed to come together and make sense, ready for its splash on the big screen.

There is quite a possibility, however, that I won't be able to find the funding for the film. This, of course, would be very, very disappointing, not only because I would have lost two years of creative work, but also my dream of visualizing this complex and exciting project on screen would be shattered.

If the project is rejected, the only thing left to do is send all the boxes of finished animation to an organisation like the Dutch Film Museum where they'll store it for the next hundred years. The possible interest of animation students looking through the animation of *Prumf* is almost nil; flipping through animated drawings without being able to see the results on film is not a very interesting exercise. Ah well, such are the hazards of being an independent artist. All I can do for the moment is keep my fingers crossed and realise that I've been quite fortunate to have seen most of my fantasies projected on screen.

During the preparations for setting up *Prumf*, the French production studio Sacrebleu showed interest in another idea of mine for a short called *What the Cuckoo Saw*. Like my film *The 2 Shoes*, the scenario is based on one of my Fiddle Fumble Stories which, in the book, was called *The Cuckoo and the Hungry Cat.*

The cuckoo story is again typical of my experiments with narrative space, a way of non-linear storytelling. In this case it's about 'leaps in time', an element of measure which, along with the use of space and the manipulation of sound and image, I designed to get the story of the young and naive occupant of a cuckoo-clock across.

In the 'Cuckoo' project, the newborn cuckoo briefly comes out of her clock every hour and tries to understand what's going on outside her hideout. She has very little time to assess the world around her when she's briefly catapulted out of her clock at every stroke of the hour.

But as the hours go by, time to look around increases and by the time the stroke of twelve arrives, the little cuckoo appreciates how much she has learned about the behaviour of a mean old cat prowling under her clock. However, she makes one almost fatal mistake…

Storyboard panels for What the Cuckoo Saw.

An early sketch of What the Cuckoo Saw.

A cuckoo in a cuckoo clock has always been inspiring to me because of the game one can play with timeslots. In another of my Fiddle Fumble Books, *Sherlook, the Cuckoo,* I told the story of a more mature cuckoo who, during her brief sojourns outside her clock, muses about a crime of passion which unfolds in the room she inhabits.

Since there seem to be endless possibilities to expand on this 'glimpses of time' idea, if I were younger, I might have considered setting up a 'What the Cuckoo Saw' series. Maybe in the next life; in this one, I am running out of time...

Four panels from Sherlook, the Cuckoo.

WHEN OLD WISE MEN GET TOGETHER

It's not only myself getting on in age. People around me, many of them old friends, are now having their birthdays in their seventies. A nice way to end this chapter might be to show the cartoon I made when my good friend Marv turned seventy. Like my films, the cartoon has a puzzle-like quality, but Marv being an intelligent person, eventually figured it out and told me that he appreciated that I had pictured myself as old and losing it like he himself (I portrayed myself on the left, the one with less hair sprouting from his ears).

This last cartoon is a card Marv sent me for my 81st birthday.

AFTERTHOUGHTS

I have some final thoughts I'd like to share with the reader of this book.

1. Animators of short films are usually hiding behind their animation desks and thus are rarely recognized by the public. We're often referred to as 'shy actors'. The only time we shine is at festivals, and although most of us are not used to the spotlight, these events give us a chance to get together and party.

2. An event which comes to mind, unrelated to anything written in this book, is that in one day, without much of a plan, I used seven different vehicles to get from A to B and back.

I started out by bicycle to go to the Montreal metro station, then took the metro to the central train station, where I boarded the train to Toronto. Upon arrival in Toronto, I rode the tram to go to a studio where I was to meet someone, and after the meeting, I took the bus to the ferry, which connects the mainland to the Toronto airport, then took a plane back to Montreal. From there, I might have taken a taxi to get back to my bicycle, which would add up to eight vehicles, but I don't remember; it's been a long time (and being Dutch, I probably walked).

3. Something else I want to mention is my appetite for reading. I read a lot, but being aware of getting older, I believe that one shouldn't lose precious time on a book which seems somewhat disappointing, so I apply a system which goes as follows:

   When starting to read a book, if one is unsure whether it's compelling enough to read all the way through, one can make a decision whether to discard the book after reading the number of pages amounting to one's age subtracted from a hundred.

   Thus, for example, when one is 20 years old, one should read at least 80 pages before one can put it aside as "not my cup of tea." When, as in my case, one is 82, one has to read only 18 pages before throwing it out without feeling guilty. When I reach a hundred, I will only have to look at the cover of the book to decide whether it's worth reading.

4. I discovered that of Gabriel Garcia Marquez's oeuvre I really only liked his bulky books, like One Hundred Years of Solitude and Love in the Time of Cholera. I was much less enchanted by his smaller books. And the other way around, I love William Trevor's short stories, but not so much his more elaborate novels.

5. For years, I have had two recurring dreams: one is that I'm in some city walking in the crowd and suddenly it starts to dawn on me that I have no clothes on, that I'm fully naked and should do something about it.

   The other one is that I'm on my way to the train station to catch a train, running late, meeting all kinds of obstacles, finally getting lost, and realizing that the situation is hopeless.

   For both dreams, waking up is always an immense relief.

   Looking back over my more than 82 years on earth, I feel fortunate to have been part of this unusual period of a rapidly changing world. It often felt like I was at the right place at the right time. Life has been kind to me.

La Voulte, France, March 2023.

FLAP
FLAP

Acknowledgements

When writing this book my thoughts kept going back to Jim Hiltz, my mentor who hired me at his small animation studio in 1964, and George Dunning, who asked me to join the team of *The Yellow Submarine.* They both gave me an invaluable introduction to the world of animation.

Many thanks to Matt Joudrey who encouraged me to write my autobiography and who wasn't afraid of my concept of sprinkling my memories with many, somewhat challenging, illustrations.

And thanks to Kiki Yee who did a very fine job of turning my English into good English.

I'm very grateful to my Canadian friend Sandra Lambert and Dutch friend Arne Westerhof who offered to proofread the manuscript of this book in its early stages.

A big thank you to Marv Newland, for our long-lasting friendship and the many wacky ideas we shared and who painstakingly went through this book to make sure that I didn't spell his name wrong.

I also want to acknowledge the National Film Board of Canada, the Eye film museum and the Netherlands Institute for Sound and Vision for their help to obtain many of the images in the book.

And, of course, thanks to my family, siblings, children and grandchildren, all sources of inspiration, popping in and out of my life.

And last but not least to my dear Diane; what can I say...

Paul Driessen drew cartoons from an early age. In 1964 he started to animate commercials at an animation studio near Amsterdam. A few years later George Dunning invited him to work on the Beatles film, *The Yellow Submarine* in London, UK. In 1970 Paul Driessen emigrated to Canada and started a freelance animation career, producing most of his personal films for the National Film Board of Canada. Since 1976 he also animated and directed many of his films for independent producers in The Netherlands. Of late his projects are also made with the support from Belgian and French production houses.

Paul Driessen has won a great many international awards for his work, including six Lifetime Achievement awards. His film *3 Misses* earned him an Oscar nomination in 2000.

From 1988 to 2005 Paul Driessen taught animation at the university of Kassel, Germany. Under his guidance his students have won two Oscars.

Paul Driessen is a member of the Academy of Motion Picture Arts and Sciences.

Copyright Extension

The author and publisher would like to thank the National Film Board of Canada for the use of archived images in this book.

OUR AT BAY PRESS ARTISTIC COMMUNITY:

PUBLISHER
Matt Joudrey

MANAGING EDITOR
Alana Brooker

SUBSTANTIVE EDITOR
Kiki Yee

COPY EDITOR
Priyanka Ketkar

PROOF EDITOR
Danni Deguire

GRAPHIC DESIGN
Lucas c Pauls

PUBLICITY AND MARKETING
Sierra Peca

AT BAY press

Paul